Love, Light, Joy & Justice

How To Be A Christian Now

Adam
Nicholas
Phillips

For Sarah

TABLE OF CONTENTS

Kim —

So grateful.

Take courage!

[signature]

I am because we are. - Desmond Tutu
Nobody's free until everybody's free. - Fannie Lou Hamer
We are hope despite the times. - John Michael Stipe

PREFACE

An overwhelming majority of American Christians - evangelical, mainline Protestant and Catholic - voted to elect for President a thrice married man who rages on social media, doesn't believe he needs forgiveness, compulsively lies and promotes legislative policy that adversely hurts those Jesus told us to care for first.

How did this happen?

That's the question many ask when we reflect on the reality that 81% of white evangelical voters and over half of their Protestant and Catholic neighbors supported Donald J. Trump in the 2016 US presidential election.

What does it mean to follow in the way of Jesus these days?

And by this question, I mean, literally in his footsteps, alongside him, and on the path he made with his very own feet some two thousand years ago - how do we follow that way?

I don't mean: what does it look like to get in the way of Jesus. These days Evangelicals and others are doing just a fine enough job doing that.

As a pastor in a time of Evangelical exclusion and trauma, I've experienced the pain, division and hate that comes with trying to authentically live in the footsteps of Jesus.

My conviction is that Jesus and those that have tried to follow in his way have always and forever been about equality, inclusion, resilient relationships, perseverance and hope.

My local church community in Portland and I paid an incredible price for our commitment to these ways of Jesus when our Evangelical denominational family kicked us out. Our sin? Welcoming and including all people. Experiencing that kind of exclusion and betrayal by people I trusted has helped me see that there are dark forces of division amongst us that aren't anything close to the way of Christ.

The same forces at play that kicked out me and my church are, in fact, the same forces at play in our politics these days. There is a choice before us between two ways - one that leads to life and one that leads to death.

We must choose life.

A community of love, light, joy & justice

I believe the real reason why Americans Christians overwhelmingly voted for Trump is because they've bought into a story about God, the world, and all of us that is nothing like the story of Jesus and his radical kindom* of love.

In a way, you could say so many of our neighbors, friends, family, and maybe even ourselves, have bought into an anti-Christ kind of story.

I'm here to tell you that the way of Jesus is radically more beautiful and better than that. But it is going to require not only some better storytelling - it's going to require that we make some key, fundamental choices about how we might live, as well.

This is a book about getting back to the roots of Jesus, who was and is about love, light, joy and justice. It's this fourfold pattern of Jesus that I believe leads us back to our true selves, together.

Love is the heartbeat of the universe reflected in Jesus - who, through his solidarity with our humanity shows us the way back to the Divine.

Light is about living for what is good, beautiful and true holistically, for one another.

Joy is found when we lean into the whole experience of our lives and courageously do our grief work, so that we might journey outward with and for others.

And Justice? That's what we're all looking for in our lives - where the world might be turned upside down and made right. Where, in the end, there is no more hunger, darkness, disease or despair. We each have a role to play in midwifing that kind of world and it's my belief that Jesus shows us a better way.

The kind of community, country and even church we're longing for doesn't accidentally happen and it doesn't come just by acts of resistance. My hope is that this book might offer some resilient ways forward.

But in order to get to the future, let's first get our bearings by looking backward to the past.

Let's go!

A quick note: I use the word "kindom" throughout this book instead of traditional "Kingdom" language. It's a subtle shift but an important intention to make sure we reflect on the kind of world Jesus was talking about - which was inclusive, reflected radical diversity and gender equality, and had no borders or walls. Also, if you want to dig deeper into what you see throughout these pages, turn to the back "liner notes" for more references and rabble rousing.

LOVE

Love is bigger than anything in its way.
Bono, U2

Evangelicals In Empire

After Donald Trump was elected President I found myself, like many others, swamped with fear, anxiety and confusion about the direction of our country. If I'm honest, I also felt downright angry that his presidency was overwhelmingly delivered by people who claimed to follow Jesus.

People that say they follow Jesus elected a man who is notorious for his racist business practices and campaign-rally dog-whistle exclusionary speeches. These self-professed Christians - often called his base - put in office a thrice-married man exposed for his noxious treatment of women, which includes having affairs with porn stars while his third wife was pregnant and bragging about getting away with sexual assault - all counter to their professed "family values." And, yes, these people known for their religiosity support a man who detains children in cages on the southern border, allies with homophobic forces threatening the dignity of all people, and lies almost every day on Twitter.

In light of all of this, the question remains for me: how might we be Christian now?

I believe love trumps hate. And I truly believe that, in the end, love will triumph over death. But the spirit of love faces some dark, trying days.

Love is the heartbeat of the universe where the end goal for us, all people, and all things is the life that is truly life. Love is about the flourishing that God dreams for all people and our planet. Without this kind of love, we fall into narcissism, nihilism, hate, suffering and darkness.

Many people think the division and discord we experience these days is a political problem. But I think it is in fact a theological problem.

Theology literally means "God-talk." And I'm convinced how we talk about God matters when it comes to living out our whole lives in the real world. For those of us leaning into the living Spirit of God - that wind behind the sails of truth, freedom and faith long-held as the third person of the Triune God - it's time to make some new fundamental choices for how we live.

This is not a new choice for us. In fact, it's one of the most ancient choices people have had to make. As we journey into the past, we will unlock some steps that might guide us along the way that have been hidden in plain sight for far too long.

Good News and Bad News

Before "evangelical" became synonymous with being part of the overwhelmingly white American electoral base that put Donald Trump into the White House, it meant something else entirely. Sometimes words matter. "Evangelical" is a word that needs to be repaired. The grammar of our faith-roots matter for the kind of fruit we all hope to bear in our world.

Originally, the word evangelical simply meant "good news." It comes from the Greek word "*euangelion*" which was used back in the day of Jesus and his first followers – but not in the way you'd think (we'll get to that in a moment). If your Bible doesn't translate this ancient Greek word as "good news" I bet it translates it as "gospel."

Which is a more modern way of saying the old English word "*God-spell*" - a word-for-word old English translation that came into usage around the 12th Century.

Gōdspel is the way English scribes translated the Latin word *evangelium* which was how they translated the original Greek word εὐαγγέλιον – or, *euangelion* which simply meant "good (*Eu-*) " "message (-*angelion*).

The way the story typically goes, in the days of Jesus, good news or glad tidings were always delivered by special messengers (literally, angels).

But quickly a word like "Gospel" became about something very different from its original intent.

We may think of it as the title of the first four books of the Christian New Testament (The Gospels of Matthew, Mark, Luke and John). Or you may think of it as a spiritual message you accepted at summer camp or in the basement of a church during a youth group event.

When thinking about the popular Christian use of the terms "gospel" and "evangelical," a pastor named Tim Keller captures the popularly held notion as something that distinguishes Christianity from other religions:

God has entered the world in Jesus Christ to achieve a salvation that we could not achieve for ourselves which now 1) converts and transforms individuals, forming them into a new humanity, and eventually 2) will renew the whole world and all creation. This is the 'good news'—the gospel.

Keller's version of the gospel may be the abiding sentiment, but I'm here to tell you that the good news is something significantly different. In fact, "Evangelical" originally had nothing to do with Jesus at all.

In the public arena, "Evangelical" began as a word employed to promote the work and might of the Roman Empire and their God-man-king Caesar. The Empire literally paid thousands of messengers to travel throughout the countryside and cities to deliver so-called "glad tidings" of Roman war stories, miracles and new births.

The great British theologian N.T. Wright describes the original non-Judeo-Christian usage of the word around "good news" or "glad tidings" as a technical term, commonly used by Roman soldiers and others to announce an imperial military victory, birth, or accession of a new emperor.

"An inscription" from 9 BCE, Wright suggests, "says it all:"

The providence which has ordered the whole of our life, showing concern and zeal, has ordained the most perfect consummation for human life by giving to it Augustus, by filling him with virtue for doing the work of a benefactor among men, and by sending in him, as it were, a savior for us and those who come after us, to make war to cease, to create order everywhere…; the birthday of the god [Augustus] was the beginning for the world of the glad tidings that have come to men through him…

But this Imperial Roman god-child, born to "save" the world was anything but "good news."

His was a way of death, destruction and slavery.
It was the way of the Roman Empire.

The first followers of Jesus knew this all too well so they decided, in acts of resistance, to be evangelical themselves and talk about "good news" as a way to subvert the oppressive, destructive ways of Empire. These first Christians talked about an entirely different sort of kindom with an altogether seriously truly true good news for all people. Early Christians lived their entire lives under the weight of Roman oppression and reappropriated the word "Evangelical" from its roots of imperial propaganda in order to shine light amidst the darkness for a better way.

The son of God has come to save the world

In 44 BCE Julius Caesar declared himself the first Emperor of Rome – which was very controversial at the time because up until that moment Rome was a Republic with a long tradition of rule by a representative body of elected leaders known as their Senate.

The Emperor had ambitions to build an all-powerful Rome

that was expansive, secure and totalitarian. He waged a series of military conquests that eventually became one grand and controversial civil war. Thrice married himself, one of Julius Caesar's lovers was Cleopatra, who was sitting on her own imperial throne in Egypt.

Julius and Cleopatra saw themselves as super-humans, and you might, too, if you had all the power and wealth they had amassed between them. They seemed invincible. They began to believe that their power alone could bring about peace and prosperity.

But one day Julius was murdered by some of his closest advisors. After a time of brutal division and civil war, Julius's adopted son Octavius eventually became emperor.

Early during Octavius's rule, a major comet was seen in the Roman sky (many historians believe it may in fact have been Halley's Comet). Octavius leveraged this moment and declared it was the assassinated Julius Caesar's soul traveling to heaven – a divine image if there ever was one.

So with Octavius the newly apparent son of god in place in the hearts of Romans, he finished the civil war and declared a Pax Romana: a Roman peace, that would be secured and maintained by him alone for generations to come.

The Roman Senate bestowed Octavius with a new title that had never been used before which sounded more religious than political. They called him Augustus – a name he invented for himself which literally meant the "Illustrious" or "Magnificent One."

In his own way, Caesar Augustus kept the peace. But it was a brutal, traumatic experience. His attendants enslaved thousands in building projects, had thousands others punished to death on Imperial torture devices called crucifixes, and taxed thousands more in the hinterlands to ensure that the peace amongst the political elite back in the Capitol was kept intact. And everyone in the Capitol bubble for generations bought into this false so-called peace because they lived in a world of denial, privilege and affluence.

With total Roman Imperial rule firmly established, it became easy for many to believe the "good news" of Augustus' fatherly divinity over them. Roman politicians and talking heads went throughout the land evangelistically, sharing Caesar's "good news" in written and spoken word. They even enlisted skilled metal workers and painters and poets to declare Augustus's god-like qualities by making images, houseware and coins emblazoned with words promoting his divinity. These cultural artifacts revealed an Empire with significant, distinct religious beliefs.

But this good news was just terrible propaganda covering up death and destruction all around.

Through slavery, heavy taxation and state-sanctioned terror, Augustus doubled the size of the Roman Empire by expanding its borders north, south, east and west while overseeing a series of massive infrastructure programs back in the heart of the empire itself – pleasing the ruling elite, stripping ordinary citizens of rights, and keeping any possible insurgents, both near and far, in check.

When indigenous folks in far off places wouldn't submit to Caesar's "divinity," his loyalist soldiers and political puppets, like King Herod and his sons in Judea, committed mass atrocities. Rumors swirled amongst the people about genocidal acts like the killing of every baby boy under the age of two in certain parts of the Empire.

One way to instill fear in the farthest corners of the Empire was to put people to death on wooden crosses, known as crucifixes.

It was a particularly heinous and shameful way to die. Rabble rousers and insurgents the Romans called "bandits"were publicly marched, carrying a large horizontal wooden plank on their backs to a location in town where they would then be tied or nailed to a large vertical plank of wood. The condemned would be stripped and flogged along the way to where they'd be hung to die over the course of a few days.

The Romans made sure that many of the victims hung low enough for wild dogs to eat their rotting flesh, left behind as carrion. What the dogs didn't eat the birds picked off for themselves. Sometimes the Romans hung one or two to die - other times it would be mass executions. Crucifixion combined the fear mongering of heads on spikes with long-suffering humiliation and public torture to terrorize their subjects and demoralize any would-be rebels. Around the time that Jesus was born in Roman occupied Palestine, people remembered the terrible day when two thousand people were crucified in a single town.

When Caesar Augustus died in 14 CE someone said they heard another person see his soul ascend to the heavens following Julius Caesar into the realm of glory. A month later the Senate officially deified Augustus and ordered the training of priests who would lead worship at newly constructed temples across the Empire. You could say that the gospel according to the Roman Empire had gone out into the four corners of the whole world.

This is the world in which Jesus and his friends lived, acted and created resilient communities of resistance.

Two Ways

The birth of Jesus by a young unmarried woman named Mary came right on time for those in dire need for the world to be turned upside down. It's a scandalous thing if you think about. The scandal isn't that mother Mary wasn't likely even thirteen years of age - that would've been normal in those days. The scandal is that this child, born in the farthest backwater corner of the Roman Empire, would come to embody a different kind of "gospel," setting off a revolution of truly good news for all people and, in his own way, subvert the powers that be.

With the birth of Jesus, God proudly declares that the way of Empire must be replaced by a kindom where love truly wins.

A Syrian physician named Luke tells the story well. Many decades after Jesus lived, this educated doctor wrote down a version of the story from Antioch - at the time, the third largest city in the Roman Empire. Luke paints a picture of love born in the world breaking down boundaries between the haves and the have-nots, including a curious collection of characters from simple fisherman, women leaders, tax collectors and Imperial soldiers who saw the light.

Mary is visited by a messenger of God named Michael who tells her that she will give birth to a special child, who will change everything forever. Hearing the news, she can hardly contain herself and breaks out into song:

"With all my heart I glorify the Lord!
* In the depths of who I am I rejoice in God my savior.*
He has looked with favor on the low status of his servant.
* Look! From now on, everyone will consider me highly*
*   favored because the mighty one has done great things*
*   for me.*
Holy is his name.
*   He shows mercy to everyone,*
*   from one generation to the next,*
*   who honors him as God.*
He has shown strength with his arm.
* He has scattered those with arrogant thoughts and proud*
inclinations.
*   He has pulled the powerful down from their thrones*
*   and lifted up the lowly.*
*   He has filled the hungry with good things*
*   and sent the rich away empty-handed.*
*   He has come to the aid of his servant Israel,*
*   remembering his mercy,*
*   just as he promised to our ancestors…"*

When you read these revolutionary lyrics, what kind of song do you hear?

To me, Mary's song sounds like punk rock, performed by feminist bands like Savages or Pussy Riot. But it's actually an ancient worship song. A worship song sung by an expectant mother looking to see the world around her turned upside down and set to rights.

We traditionally call this song the Magnificat and the magnificent thing about it is that it's a battle cry for peace, freedom, justice and inclusion for all people.

There will be no status quo any more.
There will be great change.
There will be great transformation for everyone
  - personally and collectively.

It's as if the mystery of the universe is born into the ordinary complexities of our world with a fierce, tough message of love. But not the kind of "tough love" that so many have had violently thrown at them out of condemnation. This is a tougher, maternal love that dares to believe that the powers that be of this world can be brought down and replaced with the promise of authentic, holy embrace.

Make no mistake: the birth of Jesus means utterly nothing unless it is seen as a direct referendum on the way of Empire (which is the way of death). Luke's story practically hits us over the head with it! As Luke tells it, Jesus was born during Emperor Augustus's great census who "declared that everyone throughout the Empire be enrolled on the tax lists."

It's in Luke's story where ordinary common shepherds sleeping out in the foothills receive a curious message of "wondrous, joyous news" with an invitation to come visit the newborn baby Jesus who was going to be a different kind of Caesar (or, anointed one) for "all people". The manger scene of smelly, sleepless shepherds visiting the newborn Christ who leave to become additional messengers of good news is maybe as punk rock as Mary's magnificat song - and a true reflection that God finds solidarity and belonging with those that the empires of our world would shame.

I think so many Christians miss this because they've been sold a bill of lies that Jesus was born to die on the cross so that his angry Father-God could look away from our sinfulness and "forgive us."

But according to Luke's version of the story, that's not what it is about at all. Jesus wasn't just downloaded onto Earth from his Father's heavenly courts with pre-recorded messages and a script to follow an obedient death on the cross to forgive us our sins or to start a new religion.

Jesus came to show us how to be truly human and experience the life that is truly life, reconnected with the Divine found in all of us. Which, as you can imagine, might have some real world consequences when it comes to standing with those whose backs are against the wall in acts of resistance.

There Are Two Ways

Some of the earliest Christians put together a little how-to manual on living out loud this epic new way - they called it "The Teaching" (or, *Didache* in Greek).

It's essentially an ancient manual on how to do faith-rooted community.

This teaching from the original friends of Jesus (who were known as the Apostles) contains the basic ingredients for what the practicalities of community looked like – you know, the types of rituals that mattered, suggestion on conflict resolution, and what kind of weekly rhythms to share when it came to organizing life together.

Thread throughout this 2nd century document is this magnificent saying these early friends of Jesus wanted everyone to memorize in the depths of their hearts and have on the tips of their tongues:

There are two ways: one of life and one of death.
And between the two there is a great difference.

There's a great deal of difference between the way of Jesus and the way of Caesar. The way of Jesus, as I've experienced it, is a life-giving, holistic pattern. And when living out these rhythms and possibilities, we find ourselves seeking a better way for the earth, one another and for ourselves.

The way of Caesar? It was the way of violence, hunger, scarcity and oppression.

The way of Jesus was peace - in the deepest, most abundant sense possible. Ancient Hebrew folks had a way of talking about this deep and abiding peace. They called it Shalom, where everything would be made right. With peace like that, everyone would both have enough resources to live and be able to find belonging and purpose with one another and the land, in body and soul, despite all of their divisions and differences.

The shalom of Jesus, rooted in the story of his ancestors, seemed impossibly out of this world - but he dreamed it was still truly attainable.

The peace of Christ is not just about the absence of conflict, but a holistic health and flourishing for every person, regardless of their gender, age, sexuality, or economic status. It knows no borders, nationality, political party or religion.

For Jesus there is a better way than the way of Rome - and each of us are free to make that important choice.

And that's where our story gets really interesting for those of us who live at a time where Donald J. Trump is the 45th President of the United States.

The Way of Freedom

Jesus grows up and one day, back in his home faith community, announces that everything is about to change. Jesus reads out of the Book of Isaiah - about the Hebrew Bible prophet who spoke about a suffering servant who would one day help the world reject hatred and violence and find health and wholeness.

This is how Luke remembers it:

He unrolled the scroll and found the place where it was written: The Spirit of the Lord is upon me, because the Lord has anointed me. He has sent me to preach good news to the poor, to proclaim release to the prisoners and recovery of sight to the blind, to liberate the oppressed, and to proclaim the year of the Lord's favor. He rolled up the scroll, gave it back to the synagogue assistant, and sat down. Every eye in the synagogue was fixed on him. He began to explain to them, "Today, this scripture has been fulfilled just as you heard it."

To proclaim release. Or, as the Greeks would say, *Aphiemi!*

What's amazing about this concept of *aphiemi* is that it's the same word Luke uses to talk about both "forgiveness" and "liberation." That somehow the child that Mary sings about who was born to bring about the forgiveness of sins grows up to see himself as the one to bring about the release and liberation of captive and oppressed people.

The baby boy Jesus wasn't born to just set us free from a set of bad personal sins - the Christ child came to show us all, together, how to experience a personal freedom from destructive ways and seek a collective, common good for all.

For far too long religious hucksters and con men have sold us a bill of lies - that Jesus was born to save us from sins because he died on the cross to placate an angry God. For generations we've heard this on Christian radio, read it in Christian books and heard about it in pulpits, summer camps and social media all around.

And while we've heard these stories about God's wrath and our need to be born again and ensure we're not left behind and out of the afterlife, we've been told there is only one way to vote and that there are only a couple-few issues that matter most to God: typically preventing gay marriage and abortions while denying that climate change is real.

But this is false religion - a kind of death-dealing story that has nothing to do with Mary's magnificent son Jesus. The way of Trump and white American Evangelicals is left behind religion - in collusion with the powers of death that are the empires of our day. It is time to leave it all behind.

Leaving Behind Left Behind Religion

One night at a back to school open house when I was in middle school, the adults had this great idea to have supervised play outside in the twilight of a late summer night in California while parents and guardians toured the school and met our teachers.

Sounds fun at first - who wouldn't want to play kickball with your friends or flirt with the new girl or boy near the swing set?

Somehow, though, I ended up playing Tetherball with a kid who told me all about how there was a hole in the Ozone layer above Antarctica and it was growing and getting closer to Australia and soon enough it would one day carry all of us into the sun where we would die horrible deaths caught up in flames. He said something like "even a kid wearing Nike Air Jordan's couldn't stop themselves from being dragged up into the sun when the Ozone layer bursts."

Jesus, back to school night was a nightmare!

My family went home and turned on the TV. I was a nervous wreck - but tried to keep it cool in front of my parents and sister. I just sat there during primetime television thinking how tonight might be the night where we might get sucked up into the sun and die. I was terrified.

Many years later, while in college, I worked at a bookstore called the Christian Armory. We were your one stop shop for overpriced faux leather-bound study Bibles, tracts on how to convert your Catholic neighbors, self help books on avoiding masturbation, and CDs with stickers saying "If you like Radiohead, you'll love Thousand Foot Crutch."

It was the early 2000s and we had all survived what many predicted would be the millennium apocalypse. But we were still being warned that the end was nigh and that today could be the very day where each of us could be left behind in the rapture if we weren't ready. It was a confusing time for me. I didn't grow up in the church, but sort of accidentally found my way to being a Bible thumping fundamentalist in my campus ministry group. In the end, I was doing a bad job at that, too. I liked Radiohead way better.

But this whole "left behind" business? I'd heard this story before. Sounded too much like that kid on back to school night telling me about the coming ozone apocalypse. And honestly, which one was more serious to consider?

The Left Behind book series written by Tim LaHaye and Jerry Jenkins (along with their follow up movies) unleashed a holy terror of anxiety and fear on a generation of kids, who are now adults, and made many unsure of what to believe.

They weren't the first ones with this traumatic message, of course.

At the turn of the 19th century in England and America, "dispensational" teaching began to take root where misinformed historical analysis was wedded with toxic, theological innovations describing an end times that Christians for 1800 years would've had no clue about. Thousands upon thousands of Christians on both sides of the Atlantic began to read the Thompson Chain Reference Bible which conveniently cherry picked Bible verses and read backwards into the stories of the Apostle Paul, Jesus, Isaiah and the other Hebrew Old Testament prophets a conspiracy-like theory for how God was going to deal with a fallen, broken world.

Doomsday preachers trafficked the deep south, American frontier and eventually the national radio waves in the ensuing decades telling people to prepare for the end times. The 1970s also saw two end times movies called The Cross and the Switchblade and A Thief In the Night where millions of Americans in modern cities and suburbs were indoctrinated into believing political conspiracy theories from the far right. LaHaye and Jenkins picked up the mantle and dangerously went further, reshaping American politics for generations to come.

LaHaye and Jenkins wrote these books about preparing for the coming end of the world and made millions. They then in turn invested millions on political efforts to make life miserable for women and the LGBTQ community. When they weren't making life miserable for our neighbors, they spent millions themselves to have luxurious lives in-between White House visits and the Great Beyond.

Tim LaHaye, the brains behind the operation, is one of the greatest snake oil salesmen in the history of American life. As a young man, LaHaye attended Bob Jones University - back in the days when it was one of America's most viciously segregated Christian colleges. As a pastor, LaHaye led a church in San Diego where he dove headlong into conservative politics and the work of an ex-Hollywood star named Ronald Reagan who became Governor of California with aspirations for even higher office. LaHaye parlayed all this partisan political interest into a mini-empire of influence with a group of leaders and organizations that one day became the Religious Right.

There's an old anecdote that LaHaye visited President Jimmy Carter in the White House for a breakfast meeting where pastors asked the famously born-again, Sunday school leading Democratic President why he supported legislative rights for gays and women. Carter replied that these same laws actually benefited ordinary families, too. Angry, LaHaye left that breakfast meeting and prayed aloud outside near Pennsylvania Avenue: "God, we have got to get this man out of the White House and get someone in here who will be aggressive about bringing back traditional moral values."

LaHaye found allies in folks like Focus on The Family's James Dobson and Liberty University's Jerry Falwell, Sr. In the seminal book The Strong-Willed Child, it was Dobson who inspired a generation of Christian parents to inflict corporal punishment upon their children, coming up with his half-baked theories while punishing his pet dachshund into submission with a belt. We should never forget, either, that it was Jerry Falwell Sr. who once blamed the September 11, 2001 terrorist attacks on "pagans… abortionists… feminists… gays and the lesbians."

While peddling hate and tales of the end of the world,

millions of dollars poured in, allowing these Christian fundamentalists to build empires of exclusion and hate. LaHaye, along with his wife Beverly (who ran a group called Concerned Women of America) raised millions of dollars to defeat the Equal Rights Amendment in the 1980s, preventing Constitutionally enshrined civil rights for women - furthering discrimination and inequality around pay, property, divorce and other matters. The LaHayes also bankrolled, along with the Mormon church, California's anti-gay Proposition 8 in 2008 which made gay marriage illegal (until it was overturned by the US Supreme Court in 2015's landmark *Obergefell v. Hodges* decision).

It's in this determined discrimination of the rights and dignity of our neighbors that we see how Evangelicals can get behind the election of someone like President Trump. LaHaye and Jerry Falwell, Sr. may not be around anymore - but the ghosts of their ideas continue to haunt us, especially lived out in the next generation of Christian fundamentalists like Jerry Falwell, Jr., Southern Baptist preacher Robert Jeffress, and radio host and author Eric Metaxas.

When we believe hateful, divisive religious hucksters and con-men like these, we replace Jesus's message of hope, love and inclusion with a real dread of the present and anxiety for the future.

Don't worry. We're not the first to lose sight of the priorities of Jesus. Even people back in his day would believe in false stories about the impending end of the world. Again, Luke remembers a story in which Jesus urges his friends, followers and ordinary folk to not put much stock in these doomsday prophets and hucksters.

"Beware that you are not led astray!" Jesus cried, because many would come in his name and say that the time was near for the end of the world. When people like this would come with their tales of bad news in the name of Jesus, he himself said to focus on the truly challenging and destructive things happening in their midst. It's in this moral, centered posture that Jesus says the only way forward is to leave behind the way of religion hellbent on death and choose the path of love.

Table Manners

Jesus's storytellers, like Luke, remember him talking a lot about following him. In Jesus's early days, he invited people to follow - even with a subversive gleam in his eye saying to pick up their crosses and flaunt their way of freedom in the face of Empire everyday.

The best way to follow Jesus was to imitate the way of Jesus. So his friends and followers lived out the way of Jesus in the manner he did it: befriending people whom society and the powers that be said were less than human. The way of Jesus was also about seeing and believing women, healing those hurting, feeding the hungry, and including everyone - even children, who were seemingly always excluded - and being about getting in the way of any powers of oppression, pain and death.

For Jesus, one of the most profound ways to live out this way of love for others was to sit down together over a meal and have a certain set of table manners.

One day some people were asking him what the kingdom of God would look like. (The prevailing sense was that it would come with powerful vengeance). But Jesus said it would be a great party banquet - where many would come from east, west, north and south. And the invitation list would not be those usually invited to fancy dinner parties but those left out by the privileged and powerful who ran the empires of the world. Those once seen as first in the world, would be last, and those who had been held down, kicked out, left behind and oppressed would be lifted up first. In fact, it was up to the people themselves hosting the banquet to send word out into roads near and far to compel others to come to the party.

Time and time again Jesus is urging us to break down the walls and ways in which we are not only separated from the Divine but from one another. There's inspiring mystery in Jesus's message of love. For him, it's never simply about paying worshipful devotion to God. In pursuing true, authentic love, we somehow, mysteriously love ourselves. Loving God and our neighbors as ourselves, for Jesus, was true and authentic worship which led to salvation.

When a young person asked Jesus how to inherit eternal life he didn't say that it depended on certain ways in which one believed - it mattered how one lived. And the only way for Jesus to live was to love.

And the best part about how Jesus taught this was he trusted people knew this at the core of their being, that they were innately decent, dignified and good, and that we sometimes just need help in remembering the way.

So, Jesus put the question back to him: what is written in our Scriptures?

The young person replied: To love God with everything you have and to love your neighbor as yourself.

For Jesus it was simple enough as this: choose this way of love and you will live, fully.

The empires and powers that be of this world will always lie to us otherwise. They choose the lesser way. What comes next is how we might not just resist that type of darkness but flourish, together.

LIGHT

We draw people to Christ not by loudly discrediting what they believe, by telling them how wrong they are and how right we are, but by showing them a light that is so lovely that they want with all their hearts to know the source of it.

Madeleine L'Engle

Truth In A World Of Alternative Facts

In the beginning was light. And the light was for all people. That's how John's story of the good news of Jesus begins: Naked, unashamed truth on full display.

Rather than start with a baby born in a manger in the backwaters of Empire, John talks about the great divine logic of the universe that has been real since not only before Jesus was born, but before the world was made.

"The Word," or Logos as it originally appeared in ancient Greek, is a way to talk about that which truly grounded and held together the entirety of the universe - on earth as it is in heaven, you could say.

The Word was with God in the beginning.
Everything came into being through the Word,
> *and without the Word*
> *nothing came into being*
> *through the Word was life,*
> *and the life was the light for all people.*
The light shines in the darkness,
> *and the darkness doesn't extinguish the light.*

Light is about proudly standing in one's truth aligned with the life-force of truth on display naturally all around us. I believe we know the light of truth when we see it.

John's prelude to his telling of Christ's story points back to a couple key concepts in the Hebrew Bible and helps us remember a couple things:

Namely, our original goodness as found in Genesis 1. And the audacity of God as embodied as the Woman of Wisdom in Proverbs 8.

Yeah, I know. A lot of what you have heard on Christian radio or at that church you used to attend was about how originally evil and forever sinful each one of us is and that the angry white bearded man in the clouds with a lightning bolt ready to strike is going to get us.

Nope. Not true.

In fact, God is more like a strong woman raising her voice in the highways and byways, at the crossroads of town, telling her truth that we can all return to the wisdom ways of love and justice for all people. Go read Proverbs 8 in the Hebrew Bible, where truth, justice and wisdom walk the streets embodied as a Spirit filled goddess. If it's helpful, I think it's fun to imagine a film version where the wise woman proudly parading through the streets is portrayed by Cate Blanchett, Viola Davis, Rosario Dawson or Lucy Liu.

God is not about the deathly darkness of wrath. God is about shining a light that exposes the lies we tell ourselves, the brokenness of our world, and how we might return to that original goodness that is available to everyone of us.

There Is A Light That Never Goes Out

Light. It's at the core of the Christian story. Unfortunately, many of us have inherited an alternative version of the story that we think is the only way possible. That inherited version is about the struggle of good versus evil, God versus Satan, light versus dark. It's the version of the story that starts in Genesis 3 where Adam and Eve get kicked out of the garden - forever with the curse of "bad" on their backs all for eating an apple off a tree they were explicitly told not to eat.

But the real promise for our lives is the promise that we are each fearfully, wonderfully, radically made in the image of God. That's actually right there on the first page of our Bibles in Genesis 1.

After making the earth, the sky, the sea and the animals, God gets busy one more day making humankind.

Then God said, "Let us make humanity in our image to resemble us so that they may take charge of the fish of the sea, the birds in the sky, the livestock, all the earth, and all the crawling things on earth."

God created humanity in God's own image,
        in the divine image God created them,
        male and female God created them.

What a radical statement indeed! Can you imagine everyone you know, including yourself reflecting the very image of the Divine?! That somehow in God's infinite wisdom She thought it wise to make us with the heavenly imprint, or DNA, of Her own image?

It's breathtaking stuff.

If we start with that truth, we might begin to see the rest of the story as being, and of always having been, really, really different.

What if our faith journeys were less about avoiding hell and judgement, and more about letting go of our shame and doing our part to stand in solidarity with and for the good of others?

What if it was not an endless, restless pursuit for perfection but a real return to our true selves as we were made in the first place?

What if it wasn't an endless cosmic civil war between God's angels of light and darkness but embracing the journey to walk in the everlasting love that is in fact the Light of the universe?

In the Celtic tradition, it's said that light is at the heart of all life and "it dapples through the whole of creation." The Celts - ancient and modern - reverence a church not made of hands, but washed in Divine light found everywhere in the cathedral of earth, sea and sky. Go to Iona, a little speck of an island in the Outer Hebrides of Scotland and you'll see what I'm talking about.

The great Iona pilgrimage leader John Philip Newell writes,

"In the Celtic tradition, redemption is the journey of being reconnected to the light of God within. It is a journey home

that takes us through what seems like unknown land… it is about light being liberated from the heart of creation and from the essence of who we are. It has not been overcome by darkness. Rather the light is held in the terrible bondages within us, waiting to be set free."

The light in all of us and in all things is not bestowed by some powerful empire, political party, megachurch or preacher on TV, but embodied by the One who had a downward path, helping us return to one another on planet Earth, finding our true selves in peace.

Truth and Madness

The truth is, that this promise of light and lovingkindness is not the dominant version of the Christian story today. Which has terrible, dark consequences for all of us.

Once upon a time, anyone that was so hateful to be a Neo-Nazi or White Supremacist would do it only under the cloak of white robes and the dark of the night. But today? They live in the open on social media and walk in plain daylight claiming Christ while wearing crisp polo shirts and khakis like we have seen recently in cities like Charlottesville, Virginia.

We live in a mad world. We've lost perspective on what is truly true. To put it another way, we've lost our sense of what is darkness and what is truly the light.

Ken Wilber describes this as living in an age of *"aperspectival* madness."

As Wilber says, this struggle has "indeed become the defining issue of our century, because not a single other issue can be directly and effectively addressed… there is no compass point of accessible truth to guide action in the first place. In this catastrophic wasteland, the world is now suspended."

How many times in the past month have you seen a friend or family member share an internet hoax or piece of misinformation bordering on hate on their Facebook page?

And are those internet stories posted by sensible, fact finding storytellers or just Moldovan bots on the Internet farming our anxious, tribal souls?

We're losing perspective on what is really real and truly true when powerful voices double-down on a set of "alternative facts." Instead of saying there might be differing interpretations or perspectives on a set of facts, powerful folks in high places are literally declaring, as if living in some strange otherworldly dimension, that there are not only differing points of view, but, that there are different sets of facts.

Which leads us to Charlottesville.

In August 2017 white supremacists in central Virginia, marched with tiki torches around statues of Confederate war hero and slave owner Robert E. Lee at night, chanting Nazi slogans. The next morning, in broad daylight, they paraded their violent message of hate and exclusion. All of this led to the death of Heather Heyer, out in the streets of

Charlottesville peacefully promoting love, inclusion and justice.

Her friend Marissa Blair remembered "We were just marching around, spreading love – and then the accident happened. In a split second you see a car, and you see bodies flying."

Heather was killed by a 20 year old Ohio man behind the wheel of his 2010 Dodge Challenger. This guy was known to draw swastikas and talk about his love for Hitler since he was in middle school. When I hear tragic stories of white men radicalized for hate, I wonder why nobody stepped in to offer a better story - or alert authorities.

That day President Trump shockingly said there were fine people on "both sides."

The hate we see displayed by certain corners of the church in America is not Christianity at all. It's Alt-Christianity. And like the forces at play in the dangerous Alt-Right, it must be exposed for the darkness it truly begets both near and far.

In Portland, this hate hit too close to home for us when a white supremacist murdered two men while also terribly injuring a third standing in between him and a few young women dressed in traditional Islamic hijabs. This all happened in broad daylight on a light rail train at the stop near our church. There's a version of Charlottesville too close to any of our cities and small towns these days and it's time to bring a peaceful, non-violent end to this kind of hate.

Public Theology

I don't particularly hold the belief that we are a Christian nation or that we are better than others. Most of the Founding Fathers were reaching into the words of their various denominations and traditions to put together a different form of government - one that undoubtedly set the world on a trajectory of greater liberties, peace and freedom. To that end, our nation was certainly inspired by ideas out of the wisdom traditions of Judaism and Christianity.

But many of those men weren't even Christians in any kind of traditional sense, they were Deists who believed that there was no kind of Divine flow at work in the universe at all but rather God simply wound up the world like a pocket watch and left out the back door, leaving us to figure out the rest. We're haunted still by the originators of the American experience like a lot of these Deists and Christian-types who enslaved fellow humans and saw their wives and sisters and daughters and mothers as lesser humans who weren't allowed to vote, own property or be in charge of much else than the house.

These American stories we inherit over time require that we reflect, discern and reimagine how we might live out promises of freedom and liberty for all of us in a better light today.

Perhaps it's time to remember past truth-tellers from our shared story who can help shine light again today.

With poetic, Biblical flare, a formerly enslaved man named Frederick Douglass, exposed what was wrong with the country by naming what was wrong with the religious beliefs of his age. His speeches in places like Niagara Falls and elsewhere are guiding lights for what good theology looks like in public.

Douglass wrote in his Autobiography:

"I therefore hate the corrupt, slaveholding, women-whipping, cradle-plundering, partial and hypocritical Christianity of the land [and] I look upon it as the climax of all misnomers, the boldest of all frauds, and the grossest of all libels. Never was there a clearer case of 'stealing the livery of the court of heaven to serve the devil in.'"

Around this same time, white, once-privileged women like the Grimke sisters became part of the resistance.

Sarah and Angelina Grimke were born and raised in a wealthy slave owning family in the South. They both eventually had a conversion experience and became some of the most unlikely and unknown American heroes doing their part to end racism and gender inequality. Both sisters were united in their pursuit of what they saw as a holy, Christ-centered calling for social justice, with Angelina focusing her efforts around abolition while Sarah led thousands for women's rights.

The two sisters, in the words of Angelina, literally turned "the world upside down." Locked out of smoke filled rooms where white men made society's rules and the nation's laws, the sisters turned toward political mobilization. They gathered thousands and thousands of petitions (which they called prayers!) to appeal for equal rights and access to the ballot box, healthcare and education. In 1838 Angelina organized over 20,000 of these anti-slavery petition prayers and delivered them personally to the state house in Boston, Massachusetts. Her speech before 3000 people that day was known as the largest gathering of any kind to listen to a woman speak publicly.

It didn't come without great personal cost. They were essentially cut off from their loved ones and experienced bouts of ill health and poverty. Their father was a renowned and wealthy lawyer. As a child, Sarah was known to slip into her father's study and sneak a peek at his leather-bound legal books dreaming of studying law herself. Her father denied her this wish - even though he would later admit that if she were born a man she would've been the country's greatest lawyer. Sarah's faith rooted speeches and activism for women's rights have echoes in feminist movements we see even to this day.

The stories of Frederick Douglass and the Grimke sisters inspire me to be more publicly clear about my own faith. Not like the street preachers with fire and brimstone messages and bullhorns but to be clear and simple in my God-talk in ordinary life.

A number of years ago I got a haircut by a woman with sleeve tattoos on her arms and a postcard in her hair stylist mirror that said "Fuck the Patriarchy."

This was just after Trayvon Martin was shot and killed in

Florida by George Zimmerman and a new movement was kicking off on social media by three activists named Alicia Garza, Opal Tometi and Patrisse Cullors. They declared #BlackLivesMatter. The woman cutting my hair told me she lost a friend tragically in a similar way a few years before.

That got us talking about life and social justice and the hope for better days. Right as she was cleaning up my sideburns she looked at me in the mirror and said, "What do you do for work?"

Gulp.

"I'm a pastor," I sort of whispered.

"Like, you stand up on Sundays and give talks about Jesus?"

"Yup."

"Wow, that's cool! I used to go to church but that was years ago. It just didn't feel like what I was hearing in church on Sunday mornings was relevant to the rest of my week or even what we've been talking about here."

It was weird to feel a sense of shame about my spirituality. I'm often overwhelmed by the hateful things that people do in the name of God. Sometimes I even joke that it's time to open up interfaith dialogue with my Christian neighbors - because so many days it seems like we follow different versions of Jesus.

But the more I talk out loud in public spaces about the Jesus I've come to know and the divine spark in all of us, the more people seem to resonate and have similar hopes and prayers to share. I think it's time for us to take our faith outside humbly in the light, because the little flickers of flame we each carry might help build a bigger, brighter light of intention to unmask the powers of darkness in our world.

Rooting Down To The Source

We must sift through our history in order to see what's truly knotted deep in our shared life. Embedded at the root are some horrible truths. And it's time for an excavation.

In school I read about the fight for American Independence that set all men free from the devils of tyranny. But it wasn't the whole story. I was kept in the dark.

In fact, from the beginning, America has never truly made plain the promise that all people are created equal.

America's founding documents, beautifully reflecting self-evident "truths," are also tragically flawed. The Declaration of Independence talks about our indigenous neighbors as "merciless Indian savages" while the US Constitution dehumanizes African Americans by quantifying them as merely three-fifths of a person.

The men that gave birth to the United States embedded terrible truths of racism and injustice we are still sorting through hundreds of years later. We have to reckon with the truth that decisions made hundreds of years ago affect us still to this day.

Roxanne Dunbar-Ortiz Much in her profound book An Indigenous Peoples' History of the United States details how the Doctrine of Discovery, an obscure 15th century Roman Catholic teaching issued, led to the total subjugation and pillaging of indigenous peoples in North America.

In 1452 Pope Nicholas V wrote that missionaries and secular white Europeans should:

"…invade, search out, capture, vanquish, and subdue all Saracens and pagans whatsoever, and other enemies of Christ wheresoever placed… and to reduce their persons to perpetual slavery, and to apply and appropriate to himself and his successors… to convert them to his and their use and profit"

It's shocking to see such anti-Christian teaching decreed from the highest echelons of Christian authority but then when you look at the stories of Christopher Columbus and other settlers from Europe, you begin to see history in its full light.

The dark hatred of Christian teaching like the Doctrine of Discovery was perpetrated upon the land and its native inhabitants for generations. Generations after the Revolutionary War, President Andrew Jackson exponentially carried out further injustice. In seven of his eight annual addresses to Congress (what we call the State of the Union today) Jackson called for Indigenous folks to be forcibly relocated so that white Americans could settle their resource rich land.

Can you imagine a President today singling out a group of people every year in speeches, suggesting other kinds of dehumanizing policies?

In Jackson's second state of the union, the President positioned himself as a benevolent paternalistic figure, wanting to help the "the aborigines of the country... from their wandering habits" in order to help them become a happy, prosperous people." But those were lies. His subsequent speeches revealed his true character, describing Indigenous people as "wretched," culminating in his shocking words on December 3, 1833 that "They have neither the intelligence, the industry, the moral habits, nor the desire of improvement which are essential to any favorable change in their condition. Established in the midst of another and a superior race, and without appreciating the causes of their inferiority or seeking to control them, they must necessarily yield to the force of circumstances and ere long disappear."

This is what White Supremacy looks like in our American history. Not in white hoods but in white papered policies.

We must have some hard reflections on the reality that President Trump fashions himself as a Jacksonian kind of President – going so far to make a public pilgrimage to Jackson's gravesite, hang his portrait in the Oval Office and even tweet on Jackson's 250th birthday: "We thank you for your service. We honor your memory. We build on your legacy. And we thank God for the United States of America"

Andrew Jackson's vision for America is a wretched and racist history that sowed deep seeds of sin resulting in untold suffering. It's a legacy of death that masquerades as truth today.

What would have happened if more preachers weren't like the false teachers who were decried by Frederick Douglass but more like the activistic Grimke sisters?

Each of us have a choice to make. The way of life or the way of hateful death.

One of the first followers of Jesus used to be one of the worst perpetrators of hate and violence. The Apostle Paul knew first hand what it meant to live in darkness while mistakenly thinking one was doing God's will. Known as Saul earlier in his life, he had a mystical experience on the road hunting down early Christians that forever changed his life.

In the ensuing years he leveraged his Roman citizenship (an invaluable tool in Empire) to access the far reaches of his world to spread a better message of love and light. Rather than meet darkness with more darkness, Paul urged his friends and fellow beloved ones in the greater movement to live blameless lives in the light - offering a more vibrant way in their daily, public lives.

In two letters to early Christ-centered communities, Paul encourages his broad-based community, to, in turn, live vibrant, beautiful lives seeking that which is truly true.

"You who were once darkness, but now you are light in the Lord, so live your life as children of light. Light produces fruit that consists of every sort of goodness, justice, and truth."

At the core of the earliest Christians reflections there is a constant theme of living one's life in the light and being persistently with and for one's neighbors. If we skip those parts of the story, we will remain in the dark about God's true hope for us.

Solidarity, Not Shame

Back in the 1980s there was a man in a rainbow Afro wig who would turn up at all of the major sporting events and get on TV holding up a placard that simply said "John 3:16." His name was Rollen Stewart - or Rocken Rollen for numerous sportscasters covering the NFL Super Bowl, NBA playoffs or Major League Baseball World Series.

Rollen was a born again evangelical Christian that believed his mission in life was to share the gospel with the world - particularly on the largest nationally televised stages. So he'd pinch all of his pennies together and buy an expensive seat, often near the front row, to make sure he'd get caught on camera sharing what he thought was God's light.

He held his John 3:16 sign, assuming people would then pick up a Bible and turn to the verse that said:

"For God so loved the world that he gave his one and only Son, that whoever believes in him shall not perish but have eternal life." (NIV translation)

Rollen was trying to communicate what he believed would shine a light on humanity's need to believe in Jesus. Problem was, his version of God's light was profound darkness.

During the 1986 World Series, his fourth wife Margaret left him after he choked her for standing in the wrong spot with the John 3:16 sign. Six years later, he ended up taking a maid hostage in a hotel room near LAX Airport outside Los Angeles. He went to prison, serving three life sentences. Rollen Stewart may be a profoundly troubled example of what goes wrong when we cherry pick Bible verses - but his example might shine a light for us on how we can so easily remain in the dark when we single out parts of the Bible and ignore others.

Because if Rollen would've just turned to the next verse, John 3:17, he would've seen that the whole Jesus story hinges on a cosmic commitment to nonviolence and loving care for others:

"Indeed, God did not send the Son into the world to condemn the world, but in order that the world might be saved through him."

The original context for that singular John 3:16 Bible verse is a middle of the night conversation between Jesus and a high level Jewish leader named Nicodemus. Steeling away under the Jerusalem night sky, the two have a conversation on how one might truly know God and participate in God's kindom.

Jesus says something to Nicodemus about the need to be born again (as many evangelical Bible translations put it). Nicodemus, rightly so, is utterly confused - how can an adult enter their mother's womb and be born a second time?

But buried in the ancient grammar of faith between the two is another, subtle profound deeper meaning. Jesus isn't talking about a literal second birth for mother and child.

Jesus isn't even talking about "being born again" the way you may have heard in your summer church camp.

Jesus is talking about an inner awakening that leads to outward action for others. When he talks about being born again, the concept might be better translated literally as "born from above" or figuratively as "born anew."

Nicodemus pushes Jesus to be more clear, but Jesus doesn't ever speak in blueprint formulas or Ikea furniture assembly instructions - he's not going to give anyone four spiritual laws or a nice and tidy illustration on the back of a napkin. Jesus wants to light a fuse in each of us, kindling a reconnection that our lives are somehow mysteriously but inextricably linked to divine matters. You can't blueprint that kind of awakening - you can only leave breadcrumbs. Which is why Jesus so often talks in parables, metaphors, stories, and dreams.

The invitation for each of us is to experience a second birth - an awakening - where we experience a reconnection with our unique purpose and identity and live out our waking lives in a journey of freedom and love for others.

I didn't used to believe this. I spent two years in a fundamentalist Christian campus group, memorizing 64 Bible verses that were part of a plan that unlocked the true meaning of the universe: all men had sinned and fallen short of God's plan for their lives, and since there was no way to make it right with God the Father, who had become so incensed and angry at humanity, Jesus was born to bridge the gap and forgive us our sins by dying on the cross.

So many of us have grown up with this wholly troublesome Biblical interpretation of God's wrath that we've missed the whole point of the gospel altogether.

Maybe you've heard that Father God is so angry with the sins of everyone that he sends his Son to come down to earth and bridge the cosmic divide and pay the ultimate price in his death, assuaging God's wrath. Sometimes people will tell you that Jesus took each of our places on God's death row, taking our place on the cross. The idea is that we have each fallen so miserably short of God's standards that the only way to make the world right again is to have Jesus come and die, paying the debt for our transgressions, and making a bridge from the fiery torments of hell to eternal life.

That kind of thinking is hot garbage.

God is not angry with us. God is deeply passionate about each of us.

I believe, in fact, that God is so passionate about us that in order to free us from our endless cycles of violence, fear, and debt, God came to be born in our midst in the Christ child named Yeshua bar Joseph in first century Palestine. And that little 1st century Palestinian boy we call Jesus came to be God's profound life of solidarity with us.

Jesus came to be with and amongst us, helping us see what it means to be truly human - with all of its joys and sorrows, trials and triumphs - rooting us back to the divine light that is always and forever about solidarity, not shame.

Jesus isn't about standing between us and a violent, wrathful angry father because Jesus is the perfect image - a window you could say - into the true character of God.

This is what the passion of Jesus is truly about.

If you are nervous about this kind of thinking, I don't blame you. A lot of hucksters and con men have sold us lie after lie after lie about God. All I can say is to search the Scriptures again and you will see that time and time again Jesus throws both his arms around the world in *lovingkindess*.

So if Jesus did not come to die for our sins what's the point then?

I'm inspired by how simply another early Christian puts it. Shedding light on the whole business of Jesus's affair with us and the whole world, he says it's all about love.

We know love by this, that he laid down his life for us—and we ought to lay down our lives for one another. How does God's love abide in anyone who has the world's goods and sees a brother or sister in need and yet refuses help? Little children, let us love, not in word or speech, but in truth and action.

This second John - writing in the tradition of the one who talks about God's divine light in everyone - wants his readers to know that this isn't new news at all, but the truth about the universe and us that "was from the beginning."

So why have so many of us missed this point? My friend Steve Chalke (who leads an incredible organization of Christ-centered communities called Oasis, who fight human trafficking, provide inclusive equitable education, and create community hubs) thinks it may have to do with how we read the Bible. Rather than cherry-picking Bible verses to use as weapons towards others, we might reconsider that the Bible is in fact an ancient library of books.

The Bible is not one perfect inerrant book authored by God and delivered on a cloud from heaven. The very word Bible means library. And it's a library of at least sixty-six books (if you're looking at a Protestant Bible) of imperfect but inspired stories, poetry, songs, and other teachings. If you approach the Bible as a library of books you'll quickly see some overarching themes, even while some stories within the library may contradict each other.

The overarching story of the Bible from the ancient of days is that God is in fact a God of solidarity, inviting ordinary humans like you and me through thick and thin, Empire and everyday hurdles to take the inner journey so that we might live outwardly likewise for others. It's not a story of God's wrath - that amounts to some form of cosmic child abuse when you truly think about it.

God's story is a word that says each of us can walk in the light and do our part to make sure that others can experience the light of the universe's ultimate lovingkindness.

In fact, it can be our true joy.

JOY

You got the light, count it all joy / You got the right to be mad /
But when you carry it along / you'd find that only getting in the
way / They say you gotta let it go
Solange

Forces At Play

There's a brief lesson Jesus shares that I find truly informative for what it looks like to be "sold out" for God's dream for the world.

When I was a kid "sell out" was a dirty word. It meant you and your small group of friend's favorite band went and "sold out" for a bigger record deal, somehow compromising their original vibe. But I have to say, these days I don't see being "sold out" for something as a bad thing at all. To be truly sold out for something means being all in and totally committed. To be sold out is a, "we have to wake up every morning and kind of shout it from the mountain tops kind of thing."

While digging into the parables of Jesus, and especially the interpretive writing of Robert Farrar Capon, I began to see the call to being "sold out" for Jesus in a new light.

Capon points out "two parables in one breath" that might be worth committing to memory:

"The kingdom of heaven is like a treasure that somebody hid in a field, which someone else found and covered up. Full of joy, the finder sold everything and bought that field.

Again, the kingdom of heaven is like a merchant in search of fine pearls. When he found one very precious pearl, he went and sold all that he owned and bought it."

It's about being completely sold out for the whole journey of life in the way that Jesus sees it, which ultimately is about embracing the wholeness of all of life's experiences: loss, pain, reward and treasure. The secret of the universe, I hear Jesus saying, is to buy the whole farm and see all of it through to the point of death itself, where we will find the utter glory of resurrection joy.

That began to make itself known to me one cold, wet Portland winter day a number of years ago.

Everyone Is Welcome *(Yes, everyone, right?)*

I walked out of the three-hour meeting, dusted off my boots and went home.

A couple hours later I received the news I was expecting but couldn't believe would come my way in a short email:

I was kicked out of my church family.

One of the most painful things was that the email was sent from someone I considered a mentor of more than ten years. He closed the quick email with what felt like a dagger to the gut: *"sent from my iPad."*

I belonged in the Evangelical Covenant Church for two decades, attended their camps, prayed in their congregations, learned from their pastors, trained in their seminary, raised money for their mission projects and served in five of their churches.

And in the minute or so it took to send an email from a tablet, I was tossed out.

That night at home when I showed my wife, Sarah, the news, we just stood in silence. Not knowing what else to do, we then went down to our local watering hole.

"What are you having tonight?" our friendly bartender asked. "These. Two of them. Neat. And here, put them on this card."

Pointing at the menu, we ordered two fifty-dollar shots of bourbon and charged them on the church credit card. It felt like the right thing to do sense it seemed we were drinking at our own funeral.

We sat in silence, sipped our whiskey and went home. Too numb for words. Too confused to come up with any answers. A dream was all over. We were done.

∆∆∆

Just nine months previous we had started a new church in Portland, Oregon. We called it "Christ Church" because we wanted to be simple and direct about what we were about: Jesus and community.

We'd packed up all our things and headed west on the Oregon trail from Washington, DC with the sense that we were pilgrims on a new path.

Did people in Portland need another church? We weren't even sure if anyone would want what we could offer.

Portland is perpetually included in those lists that measure which are the "least religious" cities in the country. The city has so few churches that it's easy to wonder if it was ever "churched" at all.

The other thing about Portland is that it's also on those national lists naming it as both one of the gayest and whitest cities in the U.S.

Television shows and online memes might poke fun at these facts but, for me, those statistics begged a few questions about authentic community and social justice. Where a city is so strikingly homogenous in its racial makeup, there's got to be some struggles around white supremacy and racism. And where a city is known for its gayness, there are probably some stories of others who have travelled as fellow pilgrims on the Oregon trail, too, looking for a place of love, inclusion and sanctuary.

So here we were in Portland, excited to be starting a new faith community in the Pacific Northwest but not entirely knowing how it would all end up.

One day I posted a flyer on a telephone pole in our neighborhood announcing our first Sunday gathering. It had an empty red chair with the date and time on it, including the message: *Everyone is welcome (yes, everyone!).*

That's when all hell broke loose.

A couple days later I got a call from a denominational leader who was tipped off on social media about the poster. He asked, "When you say everyone do you mean everyone?"

"Of course!" I said. In fact, I meant it so much that I said it twice:

Everyone (yes, everyone!) is welcome to join in at our first service.

"But will you let them serve in the nursery?
Will you let them play in your band?
Will you let them serve communion?"

Ah. *Them.*

I knew what this was about. I felt a shiver as if I had looked death in the face. They say the body knows what's going on even before the brain does. That was true for me. I didn't know exactly what was happening but I knew, as Melisandre says in Game Of Thrones, that it was dark and full of terrors.

My amygdala - that little ancient evolutionary honing device in our brains that the universe installed in our ancestors to run from or attack big, hairy beasts in the wilderness - was screaming "fight!" *and* "flight!" at the same time.

I was definitely in the wilderness facing two similar kinds of monsters: the beasts of exclusion and hate.

I gathered my thoughts and tried to explain in plain terms to my denominational elder that for years I had always been clear about my stance on LGBTQ inclusion, and how I even had permission from others along the way to live out my call to plant the church the way we were doing it.

Unfortunately, this guy was unmoved. He informed me that we were allowed to invite "them" to church but were expected to set up strong fences around letting "them" be volunteers, leaders or even members of the music team. We could take their money when the offering plates came around, but we could not let them speak up front or hold crying babies in the nursery.

He then proudly told this story about a woman in his congregation who brought her gay daughter to an Easter service and how, from the pulpit, he "proclaimed the gospel" and announced that gay people were welcome but they needed to get right with God. He even had suggestions for some so-called therapies that would help "repair" them of their so-called sickness.

I wanted to throw up.

Fast-forward through months of torturous phone calls, emails, text messages and face-to-face meetings, the faith family I had been part of for two decades did an unthinkable, unprecedented thing: they kicked us out in an email sent from an iPad.

It was hard to believe. I had always been upfront with my inclusive convictions while out of respect for our tradition made sure we didn't break any rules like marry same-sex couples; we thought that change could happen through slow relationship-building, storytelling, faithful work and true community.

But exclusion and hate do strange things to people. Folks

operating with this sort of scarcity mentality - that there is not enough of God's love to go around or somehow that love comes with tied strings, small print, and limitations - live in fear. That fear is what leads to false "truths" and "alternative facts."

The Bible doesn't even condemn "homosexuality." That word was inserted into English language translations in the 1940s. And any reflections on same-sex activity has nothing at all to do with loving relationships of consent - but, instead with the abuse of power.

That story in the Old Testament about Sodom and Gomorrah? That's not about about being gay - that's about how a whole culture forgot the poor and allowed fellow neighbors to experience systemic oppression.

In the New Testament when the Apostle Paul address human sexuality, like in the Book of Romans? That's about the extravagance of a Roman Imperial court run amok with lust, misuse of power and injustice all the while ordinary people suffered gross inequality and poverty. The Bible is abundantly clear in terms of human relationships: abuse of power and oppression are anti-Christ.

But the leaders of my faith family weren't interested in talking about faith or the Scriptures. They were hellbent on their policies of exclusion.

There was a rumor that I had done a mass gay wedding which was ironic because at the time, to my knowledge, we didn't even have any gay folks in our church. Our congregation was basically 20 people that had barely started, meeting in our living room, gathered around a Bible study through Jesus' Sermon on the Mount, fueled by my wife's homemade hummus, some green tea and the odd bottle of wine someone would bring.

We didn't really know how our church would survive. Especially with what happened next. A little after I got kicked out of my denomination, things started to get truly scary. Somehow people I had never met across the country got a hold of my cell phone and began calling me to tell me I was not only going to hell, but I was also leading thousands of other people to hell. Then one day emails and letters poured in threatening my life. All of this hatred, all of this violent rhetoric, spurred by one word: *everyone*.

A hate group eventually mocked up a photo of me and Sarah making us look like undead zombies, promoting Satan's lies in the world. When we found that thousands had shared that awful image one Facebook we wondered if any of this was worth it. We felt very unsafe.

In retrospect, the same forces at play at the highest levels of political power in our country today are the same forces in the larger church that were trying to hurt us personally and politically. Privileged men in power lied to us, enabled lies to be told about us and allowed us to experience not only exclusion, but many other dark, terrible things too.

This is the America we live in, where people at the highest places of power in national politics hide behind the machinations of policies and interests that peddle exclusion and death. I believe my LGBTQ family, friends, neighbors and chosen family are fearfully, wonderfully and fabulously made in God's image. But too many people in powerful places believe otherwise, which is leading to no less than literal death and destruction.

As activist and writer Kevin Miguel García says, "Bad Theology Kills." And that bad theology is held by one of the most powerful men in the world: Vice President Mike Pence.

The Vice President of the United States believes that gay people aren't ok. Pence thinks the solution is that our LGBTQ neighbors, family and friends should go get fixed in destructive gay reparative therapy. He feels so strongly about excluding gay people from having basic civil rights like marriage equality and adoption rights that, while governor of Indiana, he used the power of his pen to legislate exclusion. Pence had the audacity, like leaders in many other states, to call that kind of un-American and un-Christian legislation the "Religious Freedom Restoration Act" (RFRA).

Decisions like these by men such as Mike Pence are rooted in bad theology. Sitting with dozens and dozens of my gay neighbors around Portland and spending hours talking, and corresponding with hundreds more, I have come to see the profound level of hate and violence that bad theology instills in people, who in turn do violence to LGBTQ folk through "tough love" tactics like reparative therapy and legislative actions like RFRAs.

One friend told me how his Christian school made him watch gay pornography and electrocuted him until he collapsed on the floor and vomited. Another told me how she was encouraged to embrace older men (literally) in leadership until she began to feel physical feelings to "correct" her so-called sinful urges.

Another friend in one of these RFRA states told me how they lost rights to see their dying companion of four decades because, in the end, they were not "legal." Another told me how their parental rights were stripped and the children returned to their chemically-dependent ex-spouse, putting the children in danger.

When people in power legislate and perpetuate such exclusion and torment, other people suffer. Such decisions enable many more to act out in violent, deadly ways.

People in power have a responsibility for measured, mature and faithful protection of all citizens - not just their voters or their base. But too often these leaders provide cover for hate and violence by not using their platform for the common good. Reflecting on the increased amount of attacks on LGBTQ people, actor and activist Ellen Page went on *The Late Show with Stephen Colbert* to talk about how leaders like Mike Pence and others give cover to such hate:

"Connect the dots. This is what happens. If you are in a position of power and you hate people and you want to cause suffering to them, you go through the trouble, you spend your career trying to cause suffering, what do you think is going to happen? Kids are going to be abused and they're going to kill themselves. And people are going to be beaten on the street....This needs to fucking stop."

Sister Ellen is right - it all needs to stop. Now.

Songs Of Death & Resurrection

Music has always been a touchstone of grace in my life, so in the nights after we were kicked out of our faith gamily, I reached for my phone and started scrolling for something instrumental or ambient to help me get to sleep. I stumbled onto Brian Eno's ambient record *Apollo: Atmospheres and Soundtracks*, hoping it would take me far away from my problems for 40 minutes or so. Mercifully, it helped settle me down, allowing me to find my footing again.

The *Apollo* album is full of moody noise. It's a mysterious, dark kind of journey through unimaginable frontiers. In the liner notes Eno writes that he was trying to capture the feelings of those first astronauts that experienced the awesomeness of outer space that no one had ever seen before.

Eno hoped that his *Apollo* songs would assist others in dialing into "A unique mixture of feelings that quite possibly no human had ever experienced before, thus expanding the vocabulary of human feeling, just as those missions had expanded the boundaries of our universe."

Far from just assisting such an expansion, Apollo bore the seeds of a rebirth for me.

There's this song halfway through the record that sounds like churchy, chamber music from the future. Borrowing those downward descending tones from baroque songs like "Pachelbel's Canon in D," the soundtrack's main theme sounded like a wedding processional on the far side of Mars. Graceful, haunting, and mysterious, *"An Ending (Ascent)"* opened my heart up for me again.

I was beginning to get in touch with my grief.

I wept.
And wept.
And wept.

I was experiencing the depths of a sort of death, wherein I began to find resurrection.

This wordless song of outer-space ascent also got me thinking about a group of Psalms in the Hebrew Bible that are gathered together, known as Pilgrim Psalms or Songs of Ascent. These fourteen Psalms (120-134 in the Bible) were memorized by friends and family on pilgrimage from their towns and villages to the center of their worship and life together in Jerusalem. No matter what corner of the countryside you were traveling from, there was a sense that you were traveling "up" to a holy place on high to the Temple.

There was a sense, too, that inwardly every pilgrim, with their stories of love and loss, were also traveling up to a holy place embedded in every one of us: a place of joy. Pilgrims were each on their own path, discovering divine promises in themselves, yet they were never traveling alone as these songs were meant for community.

Such songs were about remembering past grief in order to truly find freedom and be able to choose joy.

Ancient Israel's story was not always made up of triumphant tales of exodus out of Egypt and Pharaohs' enslavement. Israel's story included the pain and tragedy of Exile. Prophets like Jeremiah, Isaiah and Amos warn God's people in the Bible of the ensuing dangers of not living in God's abundant, inclusive ways while stories in the Book of Kings and Chronicles give commentary on the various reasons why Israel and Judah's leaders fell prey to outside forces like the Babylonian Empire.

It all culminated in the destruction of the Temple in Jerusalem in 587 BCE where the people's religious, political and cultural center were destroyed. The Babylonians not only destroyed their holy sites; they also forcibly removed their leaders and artisans far away to humiliate, erase and subjugate their whole culture. It's a much longer story, but the Exile is paramount to understanding the backdrop in which Jesus would live out his life and invite others to do likewise, hundreds of years later in the shadow of another Empire in Rome.

These pilgrim Psalms were likely written in the early days of rebuilding the temple after Exile. And they were certainly on the lips of Jesus and his family and friends as they would journey every year to Jerusalem for the Passover festival when he was growing up. I like to think of Joseph, Mary, and their greater community raising their children on the journey, singing these pilgrim songs.

Psalm 126 vividly captures this inward/outward journey of pilgrims on their own path, remembering their greater, shared story while walking together with birth family and chosen family.

It kicks off with a line about remembering when God:

*"changed [our] circumstances for the better,
        it was like we had been dreaming.
Our mouths were suddenly filled with laughter;
        our tongues were filled with joyful shouts."*

Can you imagine returning to your true home after being held against your will, exiled from your people, your community, and a way which was so life-giving? Picturing myself in this story, allowing myself to be caught up in the pilgrim's journey, I can feel unbridled laughter and joy.

But it would be a joy tinged with grief. So many would have been lost along the way in those exiled days. Friends and family would abandon their own for security and for ungodly bargains with the enemy. Still more would not survive the ordeal altogether. These cries of laughter would be wedded with tears of lament and grief for what was lost along the way.

Those on the other side would find freedom sowing those tears as seeds for resilience and a future that could yield true joy.

"Let those who plant with tears reap the harvest
with joyful shouts.
Let those who go out,
crying and carrying their seed,
come home with joyful shouts,
carrying bales of grain."

When we were kicked out of our faith family, those first three days weren't joyous at all. In fact, it felt like being entombed in a sort of death. We lost so much: most of our promised three years of funding, so many of our friends and a place of belonging. But looking back at those first three days and beginning my journey of grief work, the seeds of resurrection and the joy of transformation began to take root.

If you notice in the stories about the resurrection of Jesus, after the stone of his tomb is rolled away, there is a profound sense of fear, anxiety and the residue of deep mourning. In a number of the resurrection stories, Mary Magdalene is first in line to encounter the resurrected Jesus, but she practically misses him in plain sight, as she's blinded by her own grief.

In the story that Matthew shares, she's told not to be afraid two times: once by an angel and another time by Jesus himself. The first was a messenger of God, who had a lightning-like face and wore clothes as white as snow. The angel tells Mary Magdalene and a friend to go tell others the good news that Jesus was alive.

They run away in fear and excitement. I would too if a man in white with lightning eyes told me that kind of news. But along the way something astonishing happens; they see

Jesus himself and they fall at his feet, afraid.

Jesus is never about that kind of worship. Instead, Jesus looks them in the eye and urges them, *"Do not be afraid."* *Keep going! Tell the others! The journey continues…* To the ends of the earth.

It's like Jesus is telling us to let go in order to hold fast to what is truly important.

Richard Rohr says that no transformation happens without both great suffering and great love. In the ensuing months and years, we experienced both of those in overwhelming measure.

So much about the way people share the so-called "good news" about Jesus is more about fear. That kind of spirituality is lifeless. Fear is real, yes, but if we are locked in an endless cycle of running from real life and the fear and grief that accompany it, we're never going to experience the journey of freedom and transformation Jesus invites all of us to embark upon.

I believe that if we don't do our grief work, our grief will work us. And we'll become the kind of people we don't want to become. We'll become a sort of death.

For me, the journey with Jesus is a resurrection journey that invites us to do just that: face fear, death, anxiety and grief head-on and experience the life that is truly life. That life, then, serves as a journey of joy and justice with, and for, others.

For me and my journey through grief, I was able to make some important choices towards these ends with a little help from my friends and new chosen community.

Choices

After the initial week of shock, a local television news reporter heard about our story, put a camera in front of me and asked me some questions. Soon *The Oregonian* state-wide newspaper called. Then some nationally known blogs. Then a few international news outlets.

We had made headlines.

I just kept sharing my truth and doing what I sensed was the next right thing, trying my best to stumble toward the light. I had friends along the way that helped me share my story, which we put together in a little video that went viral. People began standing in solidarity with us. Some of them even sent in money.

A pastor friend sat with me over coffee and invited us in to her congregation's historic building downtown. Soon we had new friends and chosen family looking out for us, encouraging us not to give up.

We had a meeting of our little group where we found that people were confused and entering their own seasons of grief. Thankfully nearly everyone stayed with us. People near and far not only cheered us on, but chipped in as well until we were able to raise back a third of the money that the denominational leaders had taken away.

It seemed like taking one laboring step at a time out of

survival became a sort of pilgrimage for us toward the future.

Some of us walked in the Portland Pride parade a couple months later. Sarah and I carried a sign that many others across the country have carried, saying "I'm Sorry" for all of the hateful and exclusionary ways people have acted in the name of God to the LGBTQ community. My new friend, Robyn, a trans activist and faithful Baptist, took a quick photo in the park which I posted on my Facebook page the next day. That photo went viral as well and soon my mom was calling to tell me that tennis stars, celebrities and even a website in Kenya were sharing the good news.

A European news platform blasted out our story in English and translated it into French. Within days we started receiving letters from Australia, Belgium and Senegal thanking us for speaking out and changing the narrative on LGBTQ inclusion in the church.

Far from engaging in a crusade to change the narrative, we were just trying to be faithful to our small part of the story. People started asking me if I would write a book and go on tour. I laughed. I just wanted to keep nurturing our new, fragile church community.

That's when I realized something was about to happen. In choosing to share our truth and remaining focused on our little part of the grander, more expansive story of God, I began to see healing and freedom. It's also when I began to see community really take shape.

Brené Brown says that when we "Show up for collective

moments of joy and pain.. we can actually bear witness to inextricable human connection." I knew that was true, but I was having a hard time connecting even with myself.

That's when I realized I had a fresh choice to make: the way of life or the way of death. And those days, I could feel the great difference between the two in my bones.

Henri Nouwen says,

"Joy is not the same as happiness. We can be unhappy about many things, but joy can still be there because it comes from the knowledge of God's love for us...Joy does not simply happen to us. We have to choose joy and keep choosing it every day. It is a choice based on the knowledge that we belong to God and have found in God our refuge and our safety and that nothing, not even death, can take God away from us."

Holy hell, Henri, choosing joy can be hard!

I spent weeks in therapy. Actually, I spent almost every week in therapy for three years. We had a lot of shit to work through. Why had all those people who I loved and trusted lied to and about me? Why did friends abandon us? Why was I getting death threats?

I leaned into my meditation practice - what many call contemplative prayer. That recentering helped me do my grief work as well. It took a long time, but I began to slowly feel alive again.

Getting a puppy from a sixty year old stoner dude out of the back of his Prius helped, too.

Finding our breath and holding new life, the world began to have promise again. We didn't need to burn everything down. We simply were being invited to let some things go to make room for the most important.

The late, great Phyllis Tickle wrote a powerful little book called *The Great Emergence*. She talk's about how the church goes through a sort of rummage sale every 500 years to clear out the outdated ways of thinking, believing and doing in order to make room for the better ways we'll need in the future.

In a very personal ways, we need to unpack our baggage and re-examine what it is we really need for the journey ahead. It's time to make room for some new tools, new ideas, and yes, even new friends.

 In the end, I had to journey into a profound season of both unpacking and unknowing in order that I might know what was truly good, true and beautiful again.

People did bad things to me. People do bad things to people every day. And those that commit what could be called "spiritual violence" or verbal, psychological abuse don't deserve to be in your one wild and precious life.

They don't.

Put on a rummage sale. Set them down. Let them go.

Do meditation. Take that 75 mile bicycle ride in the country. Play with puppies, let children sing to you, hike with your loved one in the rain.

Let go so you might hold fast to what is truly important.

ΔΔΔ

Later I realized that without my traumatic experience of loss and exclusion I wouldn't have been open to all of the tremendous love, experiences and friendships that were beginning to show up in my life.

As my friend Elsa says, it's people that make us what we can more fully become - whether that's in our churches or in the chosen family we journey through life with. People fearfully, wonderfully and fabulously made in God's image who walk in solidarity and not shame are the sparks of joy that help us see the true character of the Divine.

And those sparks of joy are all around us in the most unlikely, seemingly contradictory places.

The great cellist Yo-Yo Ma is perhaps best known for his performances of Bach's cello suites. I love living in a world where a boy born in France, living an immigrant life with his Chinese parents, grows up to be the genius interpreter of an 18th century German Lutheran baroque composer known for his *Ode to Joy*. Yo-Yo Ma, looking back on a career of playing the same piece in a myriad of locations, notes how the same work can carry with it marks of grace and grit, ecstasy and lament.

Referring to the *Sarabande* movement in Bach's sixth cello suite, Yo-Yo Ma told NPR's Mary Louise Kelly, "I've played this piece at both friends weddings and, unfortunately, also at their memorial services."

Joy isn't only found in the higher, ecstatic mountaintop experiences. Joy is also mysteriously found in the still, small places. Joy can be found at the birth of a newborn child and at the death of a dearly departing one. Joy can be found at the end of the marathon and in the grit of recovering from a car crash. Joy, like, light, dapples throughout the whole of creation, if we have mended broken hearts that help us see more clearly.

Jesus often talked about folks having eyes to see amidst their blindness. He's not talking about literal blindness but a kind of spiritual-metaphorical blindness. In order to have eyes to see the joy available to everyone of us, I believe we need to be present to the grief and suffering in the world and in our own lives. If we don't work through our grief, our grief will work us. If we don't do our grief work, our grief will yield a bitter harvest in our own lives that could lead to us being unhappy, stuck, and seriously unhealthy.

We have to do that grief work in community. We have to be present to our own lives and to one another so that we might be present to the world's possibilities.

And then we'll see that inner work yield profound outer work.

Remember, Jesus invites us to love God, neighbor and ourselves with everything we have. I believe when we do the courageous inner work that attends to our own brokenness and grief, we unearth death and experience the true power of resurrection - seeking love, light, joy and justice for others.

The Archbishop Desmond Tutu says: "Our greatest joy is when we seek to do good for others," and that the invitation on each of us is "To be a reservoir of joy, an oasis of peace, a pool of serenity that can ripple out to all those around you."

And Desmond Tutu knows grief.

He grew up with a beloved but alcoholic father, experiencing the ordinary everyday traumas of living in the house of one suffering from addiction. He also experienced all of that while living under the oppressive, torturous, church-supported age of Apartheid in South Africa.

Teargassed, shot at, carrying the grief of lost loved ones and friends, presiding over endless funerals of those killed by his country, Desmond Tutu knows grief.

But have you seen him dance? Have you seen him laugh? He's mad with joy, which is the experience at the far end of hard-earned wisdom. Go on YouTube and look for his 80th birthday celebration; he dances in the same church, St. George's Cathedral in Cape Town, where, decades before while preaching a sermon, white men in military uniforms with guns encircled the congregation while Tutu preached God's radical love and justice.

In the end, our journey with Jesus isn't about falling on our knees in fear, thinking about a heaven that offers no value for those of us still earthbound. The journey with Jesus is about laughing and dancing our way toward the world we long for, together.

JUSTICE

It always seems impossible until it's done.
Nelson Mandela

Getting Into Good Trouble

Hunched over, with the presence of a wise monastic elder, we had to lean in at times to hear his still, small voice as he recalled the events of over half a century before.

And then, almost out of nowhere but with great intention, he'd burst out with the power of a fiery Baptist preacher declaring:

"There's still work to be done!!"

Nearly eighty years old, John Lewis, was guiding a group, once again, on a Civil Rights pilgrimage through America's south.

I couldn't believe I had been invited to join them. I was thousands of miles away from the Pacific Northwest deep in America's South. I had joined a group of Republican and Democratic politicians and their families, a couple possible future Presidents, and a very small group of activist types. For a long weekend, we were all together as pilgrims with The Faith & Politics Institute retracing the steps of so many saints before.

Instead of visiting empty, old cathedrals in Europe, we were traversing through city streets and country roads in what Flannery O'Connor so vividly describes as the "Christ haunted" South.

It was fifty years after Martin Luther King Jr. was assassinated in Memphis and it felt like we were going deep into the heart of America's darkness in order to find the true joy and light open to all of us if we were to somehow all get on the right side of history.

We visited and meditated on holy sites where justice was sought through faith rooted, nonviolent civil disobedience. We prayed in silence where blood was shed in Tennessee and elsewhere. We heard stories from children of the movement in Birmingham and Montgomery, Alabama, whose lives were forever changed. And we marched over the Edmund Pettus Bridge in Selma where, for a moment, everything that seemed deathly impossible and out of reach, became possible.

We looked backwards over the course of those four days, in the west African tradition of "Sankofa," so that we might go forward, together.

Congressman John Lewis refuses to allow these stories to be locked up in museums and mausoleums because they still serve as touchstones of truth and conscience. For anyone looking to live faithful lives amidst exclusion, injustice and division, these living stories become guiding lights for us to find the homes and communities we've been longing for.

It's hard to believe so many generations later, but it was perfectly legal in the United States to keep kids in separate, under-resourced and unequal schools because of the color of their skin. In the darkest, most insidious communities of the former Confederacy, it was perfectly acceptable behavior for white people to execute vigilante justice by lynching men and women whose crimes were simply being neighbors who were black. And to this day, as it was in the days of the Civil Rights Movement, it is perfectly legal to deny voting rights to African Americans and other neighbors on the margins.

We have to look backwards at these stories of racism and white supremacy and the battles against them in our nation's history in order to shed light on the present day and move forward, seeking the dream where all people are truly and forever equal and free.

Back in those days, looking at the impossibility of civil, human rights, Rev. Dr. King made famous the saying that the "arc of the moral universe is long but it bends toward justice."

Calling us to towards justice out of the horrors of our own national story, John Lewis reminds us that it's up to folks like you and me to bend the arc a little more urgently and get into "good trouble" from time to time.

Rep. Lewis figures he's been arrested over forty times since he left seminary and took his theology public and into the streets with the Student Nonviolent Coordinating Committee and the broader Civil Rights Movement.

We ended our journey in Selma. Churching that morning at Brown Chapel, we sang, prayed, heard testimony and gathered around the communion table, just like those courageous ones did generations before on what became known as "Bloody Sunday." Those earlier pilgrims for social justice marched over the Edmund Pettus Bridge, into a phalanx of white supremacist Alabama State Patrolmen hellbent on violence, and everything began to change.

Back then they were marching for voting rights. Ordinary folks in Selma had organized for a few years to get the vote and also ensure their kids' lives would be a bit better in the coming years. Selma was a typical southern town in those days - with enough to go around but, because of the racist scarcity mentality of the majority of its white citizens, with immense income inequality and injustice.

So they planned a march to make things right and get into a little bit of good trouble. The beautiful thing about that first march is that it was seen as a "leaderless march." None of the big name Civil Rights leaders like Martin Luther King Jr. were able to take part. This would be an ordinary folks march with young emerging leaders like John Lewis leading the way.

Writing in his memoir "Walking with the Wind," Congressman Lewis remembers that first march in Selma having "something holy about it, as if we were walking down a sacred path."

Always prepared, Lewis carried a backpack that morning with an apple, an orange, a couple books and a toothbrush. He figured he might spend a few hours in a jail cell as he had in the past so he wanted to have something to eat and read to pass the time.

Instead, he would have his skull cracked open and left for dead on the broken Alabama pavement.

That day the Alabama state patrol was ready for battle. Clubbing men, women and children in the streets, tear gas canisters erupted while white bystanders held picnics and cheered the violence on the bridge, named after a former Confederate army officer and grand dragon of the Ku Klux Klan. This was another ordinary Sunday in America's south, where ordinary white people in their Sunday best and uniforms to protect and serve tried to hold onto their sinful, racist way of life with sheer, unadulterated violence.

Thankfully, national reporters were on the scene and the evening's news jolted the majority of the country awake, including leaders in Washington, DC.

Miraculously, no one died. Bloodied, young John Lewis stumbled along with a group of others, back to church, his backpack forever lost. They prayed and gave witness to what happened, not realizing that their story was being told in black and white on ABC News. After sharing his story about being charged by Alabama patrolmen on horseback, John felt the seriousness of his injuries and was taken to hospital with 16 others.

By the time he woke up in his hospital bed, the nation had woken, too. President Lyndon B. Johnson sent the US National Guard to protect and accompany an even bigger group of marchers who would make it from Selma to Montgomery days later. Their focused, faithful effort was a turning point pressuring the President and Congress to make forever illegal the historic practices of discrimination against African American voters. The Voting Rights Act of 1965 was passed that summer.

Now, 53 years later, we traced those same steps with John Lewis in the front of our pilgrimage march from Brown Chapel to Sylvan Street, onto Water and towards the Edmund Pettus Bridge. We were joined by thousands of others, bloggers, cable news cameras, entrepreneurs and celebrities in a sort of celebration.

But looking around the streets of Selma the morning we marched, it was hard to ignore the reality of ongoing injustice and suffering. There was open sewage in a few of the yards of homes we passed. The community's infrastructure, despite local leaders best efforts was crumbling. I was grateful for Rev. William Barber and Rev. Liz Theoharris who were in town in a parallel procession, calling for reinvigoration of the Poor People's Campaign to continue seeking unrealized dreams of equity.

Rev. Barber says there is no religious right or religious left - only a truly moral center. I think he's right. And I'll never forget the moment Pastor Barber handed Congressman Lewis the bullhorn at the Bridge - a union of past and present, calling us to keep focused on the work at hand for others.

Let Our People Go!

I was thinking of Selma when I was sitting at the gate of The U.S. Immigration and Customs Enforcement (ICE) detention center in southwest Portland. I had gotten myself into a little bit of big time good trouble. I was about to be arrested with 20 interfaith clergy.

In the spring of 2018, ICE enforcement cranked up its ferocity by implanting a "zero tolerance" policy to prevent "illegal immigration" along the southern border of the United States with Mexico. Then Attorney General Jeff Sessions, an active member of the United Methodist Church, touted this policy as a way to implement the Trump Administrations' promise to keep "America First."

But when you look at these American First priorities on first blanche, you see a troubling racist undercurrent fueling our national policies.

And no matter what anyone can say, it's indefensible to separate children from their families and put kids in cages in detention centers. For me, it's the immoral, yet internally consistent, conclusion of a society that thinks there are perfectly fine people amongst the white supremacists who walked the streets of Charlottesville in their khakis and polo shirts. Normalizing that kind of hate enables legislative decisions that harm and kill kids. And Jesus has nothing to do with that other than to turn the tables and get arrested.

President Trump has raided millions of US taxpayer dollars from programs to help national security and disaster relief and he reappropriated those funds so he could lock up children. Thousands of kids have been placed in government contracted detention centers. They're running out of room and looking for upwards of an additional $1 billion in funding to keep people out and families split apart.

My friend Phillis Sheppard, a womanist theologian now at Vanderbilt, once taught me the old adage that if we're pulling babies out of rushing rivers, it's mandatory we go up-stream and see why they are coming this way in the first place. Separating families at the US-Mexico border doesn't get anywhere near addressing the reasons why people are putting their lives in danger looking for a better way.

Much like the Alabama state patrol and the once legal segregated American south, the tactics of ICE agents and our federal laws are morally bankrupt. It's time for a major change.

So, a group of us decided to sit down and pray for that change.

With a few hundred others, our prayer service opened with two pieces of good news: Albert, a Cameroonian man, had been released the day before from a federal penitentiary in rural Oregon. For months he sat in the Sheridan federal prison, wondering alongside hundreds of others if he'd ever see the light of day again.

We also heard how Luis, a father of two young children, was reunited with his family after being separated from his wife and kids on the southern U.S. border and thrown into a cold freezer cell for hours.

As we continued praying, singing and sharing stories, we could see squad cars surrounding us and agents putting on tactical gear. I wondered what the officers were thinking as they prepared to make arrests. I noticed two taking a selfie in the wings before they came to arrest us. A feeling of anger welled up inside me.

They took all 20 of us back behind the ICE gates into a holding garage and processed us one by one – placing our belongings in plastic bags while turning us around and handcuffing us with plastic ties. My colleague next to me asked one of the officers why he was wearing a balaclava covering all but his eyes. He said that previous protesters took photos of him and hunted him down in his neighborhood, harassing his spouse and two kids – both under the age of 6. In conversation, we learned one of the other officers attended my rabbi friend's synagogue as a young boy. It was these small moments of humanity that made me realize that, despite our lament and anger at inhumane policies, that we're all part of one bigger human family. My anger diminished into profound lament.

Half of our group was immediately ushered into a van downtown where they were quickly processed. But the rest of us were left behind and held in ICE cells for the next three hours. We were separated by gender, with our female colleagues placed in the "Women's" cell and the six of us remaining men placed in the juvenile cell. They wouldn't put us in the "Men's" cell as two Latino men were already there, waiting to be processed and sent up to the detention center in Tacoma, Washington. We eventually saw them marched out in metal shackles.

Sitting there in the juvenile cell, I wondered why we were given different treatment with our plastic handcuffs. And I also thought of all the young people that had been previously detained in that cold cell where I now sat, with the metal toilet in the corner under incredibly-too-bright fluorescent lights. I quietly said a prayer for them, feeling like our efforts, while maybe meaningful in the moment, were too late for them as they remained detained and separated from their loved ones and communities.

I went home that night and had a glass of wine with my wife and tucked my toddler son into bed in the warmth of our own home. My choice to get involved in some good trouble that day was short-lived compared to the ongoing, seemingly unending, suffering of those for whom we were seeking justice. Trump's heinous zero tolerance policy continued unabated - with the shocking tear gassing of children and the death of a detained seven year old from Honduras named Jakelin in the weeks leading up to Christmas.

It seemed like our government was forcing us to relive King Herod's ancient threat to slaughter the innocents all over again around a holy season.

Holy Urgency!

The Gospel of Mark - the earliest account of Jesus life on earth - doesn't include any Christmas birth miracles and originally didn't have anything to say about his resurrection. It begins with urgency and ends with a continued, deadly sense of urgency.

Many believe that Mark was writing around the time of Emperor Nero's great persecution of Jews and Jewish Christians. There's an old story where the over-indulgent Nero played the fiddle while the city of Rome burnt to the ground in the great fire of 64. There were always salacious tales of his opulent parties and lascivious behavior and it began to take a toll on his support amongst the ruling classes. So, after the fire, and needing scapegoats to blame, Nero went on the attack - rounding up and killing Jews and Jesus followers alike by hanging them on thousands of crucifixes. This led to a great and violent Jewish resistance that continued after Nero's own death in 68. In the end, the Empire's policies of death and destruction continued with the sacking of Jerusalem and the people's Temple.

It's with this backdrop of hell on earth that Mark wrote about Jesus's call to ordinary everyday folk to pick up their cross and follow him. In the opening lines of Mark's story of Jesus, fishermen drop their nets and follow the one who proceeds to go on a journey of healing, reconciliation and justice for those the Empire had long since forgotten about.

Time and time again Jesus encounters religious elites who charge Jesus with breaking the law - seditious acts against both religion and empire alike. The authorities see Jesus's acts of healing, resistance, and table manners (eating with "sinners and saints" alike from all walks of life) as seditious attempts to upend the status quo.

Jesus was, in fact, on an urgent mission to do just that - seek great transformation of the world around him. But it wasn't just political subversion Jesus was after - he was looking to upend our own personal status quos. He was offering ways to pray, find personal healing, and celebrate community, despite the Empire's attempts to colonize the land and people's psyches.

Casting out demons and darkness all along the way, Jesus barely has time to offer any words of wisdom. Constantly on the move, he offers parable stories so that people could share them amongst themselves and with others they'd encounter along life's way. Some of his most well known were parables of the kingdom of God - which, would not be brought about by political and social violence, but with people conspiring with the land to cultivate a mighty crop in small, forgotten places.

The parable of the Mustard Seed captures in vivid, simple detail the hope of the earth bearing fruit for holy habitation - including all the birds of the air to find home and security.

In the final analysis, Jesus is absolutely about justice. He wants us all to find home and security.

Does Jesus Have a Half Brother Living in Mom's Basement?

I'll never forget the day a Catholic priest named Father Michael Pfleger came to preach at our little evangelical seminary on the North Side of Chicago. For four decades Fr. Pfleger has led the Faith Community of Saint Sabina's - the nearly all black Catholic parish on Chicago's South Side. Pfleger is white - like German American white. The first time I saw him he reminded me of my grandfather - an eternally youthful, diminutive, kindly fellow with his hair sort of gel creamed over in a slight but distinct part. That was, until I heard him preach.

Fr. Pfleger preaches like he's straight out of a Johnny Cash inspired dystopian graphic novel with the sonorous voice of a black Baptist preacher come to tell us all to get right with God or else we'll have hell to pay. It feels like a turn or burn kind of sermon. But it's a distinctly different kind of turning and a different kind of burning he's goes on about.

The German American, Chicago born and raised priest made a name for himself protesting the Jerry Springer show with his flock in the Nineties for its degrading depiction of women and on-stage fights. It was definitely the kind of story local news liked to run with, but Fr. Pfleger was not just preaching against amoral television hucksters, he was about much more than that.

Fr. Pfleger was preaching a fierce urgency of seeking the kindom of God, now. And that fierce urgency meant fire Sunday preaching as well as taking to the streets to call people out to live a better way.

To this day, Fr. Pleger is one of the nation's fiercest anti-gun critics, taking his God-talk to the streets to denounce how his beloved city of Chicago has suffered more deaths by gun violence than many war zones. Kanye West has called his hometown *Chi-raq* for a reason. (In Spike Lee's 2015 movie *Chi-raq*, which addresses the city's tragic gun violence, Pfleger inspired the character played by another great Chicagoan, John Cusack.)

He preaches redemption from social sin and victory in personal journeys. Once a three-pack a day smoker, Pfleger is known for his faith-rooted commitments when it comes to healing and addiction. He's been known to preach that "God didn't deliver you from cocaine and alcohol so you could be addicted to nicotine… God loves you, God loves you!"

He's been arrested for speaking out against Apartheid in South Africa, US drug policy, and so much more. People label him an "Activist priest" - a member of the so-called Christian Left. But anyone that's been to mass at St. Sabina's, greeted by an enormous altar piece of a black Jesus reaching out his hands to welcome all people into his divinely human embrace, will tell you that Fr. Mike is just a damn good pastor. He lives in the neighborhood, he's known in the neighborhood, he laughs and weeps with the neighborhood. A father himself through adoption and foster parenting - Pleger lost his son Jarvis to unprovoked gun violence in 1998.

So one day Fr. Pfleger came to share about Jesus to a bunch of mostly white suburban-raised seminarians at our evangelical chapel. President George W. Bush had made the case for invading Iraq, genocide was unfolding in the Sudan, and our city was rapidly gentrifying, pushing out neighbors of color from their homes to make way for new condos and coffee shops for more affluent white folks. Chapel was full that day - we were eager to hear what the preacher had to say.

A member of the faculty got up to introduce Fr. Pfleger by saying that he was "our kind of guy" because "he believed in Jesus *and* Justice." I looked over to my friend and muttered under my breath - who's this Justice character?

Seriously: Is Justice the half-brother of Jesus who still lives in Mom's basement? We all know the type. Justice is probably up way too late at night vaping and on Reddit talking about how *Black Mirror* isn't just a television show on Netflix but happening right here, right now in real life. Justice doesn't have much on his schedule during the day other than showing up at protest marches and meeting up with fellow activists for a pour over coffee and a cigarette. Justice couldn't tell you one thing about the latest Contemporary Christian Music album lighting up the worship charts but he can give you an in-depth analysis of Kendrick Lamar's *Damn*. Justice is an alright enough dude - we just don't know if we want him showing up at the church BBQ because he might have some awkward things to say.

Thankfully Jesus and Justice aren't two different people at all - but intimately the same.

Justice is about the restoration and right-setting of all things. Justice repairs structures and scenarios that may make it possible for people to be in right relationship. Justice is about turning the world upside down so that it might be made right.

I think part of our problem as Christians is that we've been taught a schizophrenic kind of Christ. We know the Jesus who heals the hurting and who died on the cross but a lot of us were told not to make too big a deal out of Jesus turning over tables, disrupting a marketplace rife with inequality, and speaking about release of the captives and the oppressed.

This Is Not The End, This Is the Revealing

When we look at our present moment, there seems to be an overwhelming volume of issues that demand justice.

In his own day, the Reverend Dr. Martin Luther King said that there were three ghosts haunting American life in the 1960s:

> 1) endless wars like Vietnam,
> 2) emerging income inequality and dire poverty in urban cities and rural landscapes, and
> 3) Jim Crow legislation that replaced slavery with another vile form of oppression and hate.

These three evils revealed a sort of apocalyptic nightmare instead of the peaceful pastoral American dream. And shining light on these three evils allows for the expression of wounds - which is integral on the path to healing.

If only we could learn from past history. Because America's three evils of endless militarism, income inequality, and racial equity are still on the rise with even new, perhaps more dire challenges.

Reflecting on Jesus' call to discipleship in the 21st century, Ched Myers concludes that "we continue to live in apocalyptic times. But today the three specters famously named by Dr. King a half century ago—war, poverty and

racism—have been joined, and perhaps even overtaken, by a fourth horseman of the apocalypse: climate crisis."
Ched Myers is right. Climate Change is real. And it adverserly effects our most vulnerable and marginalized neighbors first and worse.

Look at the series of devastating weather patterns from hurricanes to tornadoes, floods, blizzards and heat waves that have cause untold trauma, destruction and despair in the last number of years. This is why it was so devastating that the Trump Administration pulled us out of the Paris accords. We need more sensible policy when it comes to rolling back the climate crisis than less.

Honestly, we have our work cut out for us.

Why do we settle for a world where the top 1% own over half of the globe's wealth while the bottom 70% of working folks receive less than 3%? Something is desperately wrong. It's not socialist to demand that the world's wealth be shared more equitably for all of us. It's Christian.

We must firmly reject, too, the kind of horrors that women have suffered in the workplace, on campus, at home and even in churches. The #MeToo and #ChurchToo movement is unravelling generations of misogyny and sexual violence - it may yet flip the world on its head where history evolves into a collective *herstory* of wholeness. But it will take courage, tenacity, and individual-meets-systemic verve.

Persistent education inequity, where poor children and especially children of color, are locked out of opportunities while kids fortunate to be born in upwardly mobile communities get vouchers and access to greater potential? It's time to demand all kids get fully equitable education opportunity - and even those most at risk of being left behind in education, we must expect greater focus and effort.

And it's time that we demand action on sensible gun control. How many of our public places, once reserved for joy and community, must be sacrificed in the name of gun rights? Our schools, cinemas, ballparks and everywhere far and wide, including our places of work and home must be sanctuaries rather than theaters of war. Thankfully it's high school kids from places like Parkland, Florida that are acting like the real adults out there - urging us beyond thoughts and prayer and into action.

It's time to stand in radical solidarity with all people, seeking an end to white supremacy. Which means not only tearing down memorials to a slave-trading past, but affirming that Black Lives Matter through a radical overhaul of public policies, as well as a radical repair of our human hearts. We must no longer build walls to keep people out of our communities and country based on the color of their skin or religion.

It always seems impossible until it's done.

Jesus invites everyone of us to contemplate such dreams, and awaken one another to act.

Radically Returning to Us

We have to get back to basics when it comes to our life and faith together.

When we root down to the source of all things, I believe we might begin to return to the way each one of us knows we can be, both when we are present to one another and when we are present to our own hopes, yearnings, and dreams.

The way forward is not the deathly, divisive and destructive ways of old doctrines and dogmas of fear, exclusion and hate. The way forward is the way of life, as those early Christ followers shared in the *Didache*, which truly yields love, light, joy and justice.

Jesus isn't concerned about dead doctrines we might sign our life away to on some piece of paper and store away in our brains. Jesus is about a heartbeat lived faith that bears fruit for others and ourselves.

It's time we leave behind the old ways in order to recover the ancient ways. The future for all of us and our planet depend on it.

I was awakened to this when I was visiting a pepper field and rice patty in rural Thailand. I was with some friends who talked about Jesus a little bit differently. But it was how I always knew Jesus in my gut!

Gathered with a small group of fellow pilgrims from around the world, we heard stories of transformation in their communities back home, while we labored together picking peppers and planting rice in flooded plains in backbreaking labor, earning pennies a day. It was this pilgrimage of sorts that helped me see that *how* we believe roots us in how we might truly live.

We sat around plastic tables those humid nights over cold beer and sodas, and my new British friends Steve Chalke, Dave Parr and Jill Rowe at Oasis taught me a five-fold rhythm that has the potential to transform everything. They call it living a Christ-centered ethos of equality, inclusion, relationships, hope and perseverance. They are now tattooed on my heart, and are the core values I carry with me each day.

Ethos refers to a kind of lived belief rather than merely a brain-held dogmatic belief. Today, we use this ethos to guide our Christ-centered community in Portland:

A desire to treat everyone equally, respecting differences
A passion to include everyone
A commitment to healthy and open relationships
A deep sense of hope that things can change and be transformed
A sense of perseverance to keep going for the long haul

What I love about this ethos is that it's something ordinary neighbors from all walks of life can come together and rally around.

Yes, these are deeply Christ-centered beliefs. As I have rooted down around each of these five values, I see Jesus at work, which helps me find his ancient away with fresh vision today.

God made all people *equally* in God's image. Jesus radically lived this out by centering his time with those that the world deemed outcast.

And God counts all people in, unless they want to be counted out. Jesus was always on the move, and throughout the seaside, country and city all sorts of people would come and go, experiencing full *inclusion* from the margins to the center and back again.

God is profoundly about healthy, interdependent *relationship*. No matter how you square it in the tradition of Jesus, the image of God the Creator, Christ and Spirit is a never ending circle of care and trust, with an open table for us to join in.

And the story about Jesus is the promise that life triumphs over death. That *hope* is stronger than mere well wishes. Resurrection matters for our everyday living. The data may look grim, the situation may be dire, but all things can be transformed. As Jim Wallis says, "hope is believing in spite of the evidence, and then watching the evidence change."

In life we *persevere* by finding ourselves in a bigger communion of sinners and saints through the long arc of history. We stand on their shoulders, we expand our understanding and consciousness and we are able to see a bit more clearly through the fog of life's way.

At the heart of all things, I believe everyday people are looking for purpose, belonging and thriving for all. Living out an ethos of equality, inclusion, relationships, hope and perseverance is not a monopoly of the left or right, believers or skeptics. It's the character held at the center of all of us that might still believe in the potential of transformation and the common good.

Even the most heinous, hateful, awful people? Yes. I can't explain the dark mystery that animates some folk to act the way they do. Perhaps they've been deceived or have experienced a deep trauma themselves; they've chosen to recycle their wounds and ignorance back into the world on others. The task for us is not to tear them down but to show up and let our life shine brighter.

It's time to return to the way of life. It's time to live lives that are full of love, light, joy and justice. It's time to work together to build the kind of world we've been waiting for. Let's do it together.

I'm Dying To See How This One Ends
a postscript

Back in December 2014, Melania Trump posted a video on her Facebook account that I find surprisingly compelling. Melania, in the back seat, films her husband, who is behind the wheel driving, and had yet to announce his run for President, with their son sitting up front blaring music on their way home. What were they listening to? Taylor Swift's new-at-the-time single "Blank Space," from her wildly popular and wonderful album 1989.

It's an endearing 19 second glimpse into what ordinary, everyday American families do all the time - listen to fun music, creating memories on the freeway heading home from a family dinner out.

Melania captioned the Facebook post:
"Fun night with my two boys DJT & BWT 🖤"

For me it is a good touch stone to remember the humanity of individuals we're dealing with and standing up to in the midst of terrible, divisive times.

I worry that in standing up for love and doing what's right, we may inadvertently become the kind of people we're trying to overcome.

How might we remain inclusive while not excluding adversaries? Don't get me wrong - I believe the policies and actions of President Donald Trump and Vice President Mike Pence are deeply dangerous and in stark opposition to the way of Jesus. What they are about hurt people. I truly believe their way is a way towards despair for most people.

But what if they were to change their ways, and, in the words of Jesus, "repent?" What if Donald Trump went down to El Paso and called a press conference admitting his immigration policies were wrong and he was going to immediately reverse them after hearing about another child who died in US custody (as of this writing 6 immigrant children have died - more than the previous 10 years combined).

What if Mike Pence received a phone call from a gay relative or school-age friend that helped change his mind and reverse his ghastly stance on LGBTQ rights?

What if?

I don't think we should wait for these what if's. I believe we need to stand up, organize, mobilize and do every thing we can to get these men out of office and send them packing for the footnotes of world history.

But it's good to remember that who we're dealing with are human beings, somehow also mysteriously made in the image of God. And that these leaders are part of a greater terrible system of powers and principalities of oppression and division.

In living well for the common good how might we shine a light while indeed breaking the wheel of dehumanization and violence once and for all?
We need to dig deep in how we act for change. We also must examine how we use social media, how we relate to others in real life and how we simply, daily behave while we're trying to build that world of belonging and justice we know is within reach if we seek the authentic way of Jesus.

I'd like to think we can stand up to tyrants, liars, bullies and hucksters in non-violent acts of love rather than burn everything and everyone down in fiery rage.

It serves us well to remember that "We aren't fighting against human enemies but against rulers, authorities, forces of cosmic darkness, and spiritual powers of evil in the heavens. (Ephesians 6:12)."

Trump and Pence, horribly misguided and flawed men alike, are simply symptoms of a greater disease tormenting all of us. Their actions and beliefs disqualify them as leaders, certainly. But the past few years have only revealed that if they are no longer in power, someone else from their ranks (maybe even smarter and stronger) will simply take their place.

The first friends of Jesus knew this reality all too well. They knew that in living for love and light amidst the powers of imperial Roman darkness, they were up against almost invisible powers. In the face of such evil and darkness we are in the fight for our lives.

So let's not simply resist well. Let's live lives of resilience along the way - which is a greater, more worthwhile endeavor.
 In the end there are no shortcuts to the way dreamed up by Jesus and his first friends. There is only the long, intentional route to freedom.

∆∆∆

The liner notes

This book originally started off as a 300 page screed written during the Oregonian snowpocalypse of January 2016. A lot was happening in my life and in the country. It felt liberating to both vent and then walk away from that and breathe - to get in touch with my own grief. That's when the section on joy began to emerge and the book took its turn to what you have today. I want to recognize this is not an academic work by any stretch. My hope is that partly through manifesto and memoir I might help others put words to their own experiences and journey.

When I was young I used to love combing through album liner notes of some of my favorite bands. It's how I first learned about human rights, women's rights, anti-racism, ending extreme poverty and caring ecologically for our planet. Those albums are probably one of the main reasons I eventually became a pastor as well as worked for a great organization like the ONE Campaign to end extreme poverty and HIV/AIDS. Hopefully these notes will help point you to some of the ideas behind my words and how you can go from here to be more informed and involved.

All scripture quotations, unless otherwise noted, are from the Common English Bible (2011), which I find to be one of the freshest, most inclusive translations out there right now. If you're looking for a copy for your smartphone or tablet, download the app "Our Bible" for free.

LOVE

"Love Is Bigger Than Anything In Its Way" is from U2's 2017 album Songs of Experience. Bono shares more about love, mortality, faith, politics and even the Apostle Paul in his December 27, 2017 *Rolling Stone* Interview.

Evangelicals In Empire

Read "An Oral History of Trump's Bigotry" by David A. Graham, Adrienne Green, Cullen Murphy and Parker Richards in the June 2019 issue of the *Atlantic*.

If you'd like to go deeper on the idea of Jesus & Empire, check out Wes Howard-Brook's amazing book *Come Out, My People! God's Call out of Empire in the Bible and Beyond*, another book by John Dominic Crossan called *Jesus: A Revolutionary Biography* and the audio recording *"A Revolutionary Christmas: Live at the Largo, 2015"* by Rob Bell.

I came across Tim Keller's description of "evangelical" in a piece called *"The Gospel: Key To Change"* which I found on this website: monergism.com/gospel-key-change. Tim Keller, founding pastor of the influential Redeemer Church in New York City is an incredible and sincere Christian leader. I just find him completely, sincerely wrong when it comes to LGBTQ matters and his uncritical embrace of Trump political allies and friends like Veggie-Tales writer Eric Metaxas. That said, his book *Prodigal God: Recovering The Heart Of The Christian Faith* is breathtakingly good and still informs my understanding of the heart of God today.

The part about the "Priene Inscription" I first found in NT Wright's accessible little book called *What Saint Paul Really Said: Was Paul Of Tarsus The Real Founder Of Christianity?*

You can't go wrong with Mary Beard's excellent *SPQR: A History Of Ancient Rome*. Two must read early church history books are Justo Gonzalez's *The Story of Christianity* and Diarmaid MacCullouch's *Christianity: The First Three Thousand Years*. There's also a great book that imagines what daily life was like choosing to be a Christian in Imperial Rome by Brian J. Walsh and Sylvia C. Keesmat called *Colossians Remixed: Subverting The Empire*.

Two Ways
You can access the *Didache* online or in a collection like *Documents Of The Christian Church: New Edition* edited by Henry Bettenson & Chris Maunder.

The kid at tetherball on back to school night failed to tell me that back in 1987 world leaders signed the Montreal protocol to eliminate chlorofluorocarbons and other chemicals found in products like canned hairspray that were causing real deal damage to our atmosphere. Climate change is real and we must do things, like support broad-based global solutions with others. This is, in part, why Trump leaving the Paris Climate Accords is so disastrous for the health of our planet.

Mary's Magnificat can be found in Luke 1:46-55

Jesus warned about religious hucksters proclaiming the end was nigh in Luke 21:8, 9

Jesus invited folks to pick up their cross and follow him in Luke 9:23

Read about Jesus's table manners in Luke 13-14

Leaving Behind Left Behind Religion

For more on the rise of LaHaye and the Religious Right, including Billy Graham's influence and the emergence of our modern day Reagan-rooted Conservative Politics, please read Darren Duchuk's *From Bible Belt to Sunbelt: Plain-Folk Religion, Grassroots Politics, and the Rise of Evangelical Conservatism.*

Also, for what it's worth, LaHaye's coauthor Jerry Jenkins confessed about his own gambling addiction and was later edged out of a luxury penthouse his family illegally occupied at Moody Bible Institute, a violation of Illinois state law.

What has happened to Eric Metaxas? He went from an interesting children's storyteller (ahem, Veggie-Tales) to becoming a mean apologist for Donald Trump. If you've read Metaxas's popular biography on Dietrich Bonhoeffer, please rectify that soon by checking out *Strange Glory: A Life Of Dietrich Bonhoeffer* by Charles Marsh. Bonhoeffer may be one of the most important white Protestant male theologians for this time and we must remember his life and legacy well.

Jesus invitation to "the three loves" is so important it's found in three places in the Bible: Mark 12.28-34, Matthew 22.34-40 and Luke 10.25-28

LIGHT

Madeleine L'Engle quote on light is in one of my favorite books of all time, *Walking On Water: Reflections on Faith And Art.*

Truth In A World Of Alternative Facts

The Word that was life and light for all people is from John 1:1-5. The Biblical story - or poem, really - about humanity being made in God's image is centered in Genesis 1:26, 27.

If you are looking to dive deeper into the Celtic wisdom tradition please read the kind and profound John Philip Newell of Edinburgh. Start with *Listening for the Heartbeat of God: A Celtic Spirituality* and eventually get to *The Rebirthing of God: Christianity's Struggle for New Beginnings.*

For more on *"aperspectival* madness," read Ken Wilber's accessible and excellent book *Trump And a Post-Truth World.* Marissa Blair's quote about the death of her friend Heather Heyer was found in the August 13, 2017 *New York Times'* article "Heather Heyer, Charlottesville Victim, Is Recalled as 'a Strong Woman'" by Christina Caron.

Public Theology

For more on Deism read *Faiths of Our Founding Fathers* by David L. Holmes. And check out Mark Noll's excellent *America's God.* Please purchase a copy of *A Narrative of the Life of Frederick Douglass* by the great man himself and return to it often. For more on the Grimke Sisters, check out Mark Perry's *Lift Up Thy Voice: The Sarah and Angelina Grimke Family's Journey From Slaveholders to Civil Rights Leaders.*

As you read Roxanne Dunbar-Ortiz Much book *An Indigenous Peoples History of the United States*, also look for the work of Mark Charles at wirelesshogan.com. And for more on American history, I highly recommend Jill Lepore's

These Truths: A History of the United States, and *Myths America Lives By: White Supremacy And The Stories That Give Us Meaning* by Richard Hughes.

The Biblical quote about "those who once lived in darkness" by the early Christian leader known as the Apostle Paul is found in Ephesians 5:8,9.

Solidarity, Not Shame

The best place to find more on "Rocken Rollen" is actually in his Wikipedia entry.

The Biblical verses about "We know love by this" is from1 John 3:16-18 - I use the NRSV translation. 1 John 1:1 also talks about light from the beginning.

Get to know Steve Chalke's inspiring work at http://openchurch.network - and be sure to watch his "Chalke Talk's" on the Bible or read his essay on "Taking The Bible Seriously."

JOY

The lyric about light and joy is from a song called "Mad" on Solange's masterpiece 2016 album *A Seat At The Table.*

Forces At Play

The parable(s) about being sold out for the kingdom of can be found in Matthew 13:44-46. The best book I know about the parables of Jesus is the magnificent *Kingdom, Grace, Judgement: Paradox, Outrage, and Vindication in the Parables of Jesus* by Robert Farrar Capon (who was also an incredible food writer, too!).

If you want to learn more about our story, check out my TEDxMtHood talk "Inclusion: The Ancient Idea That Just Might Save All Of Us," a video short directed by Zach Putnam and featured by the *Atlantic* and archived at zachputnam.com and Kevin Eckstrom's *Religion News Service* story "Evangelicals Pull Support For Portland's Christ Church And Pastor Adam Phillips Over LGBT Stance" which was published on *HuffingtonPost.com, The Washington Post* and elsewhere in February 2015.

The ECC also pushed out my friend Andy Goebel and the church he founded the same day. Andy's story is a powerful one of resurrection and rebirth, as well - his church eventually merged with a neighborhood United Methodist Church and are doing profound things with the houseless community to provide shelter and affordable housing. You should check out Portsmouth Union, co-founded by pastors Julia Nielsen and Andy Goebel for a radical and simple model on what it looks like to do church in the 21st century for the common good.

The $50 whiskies were Pappy Van Winkle and the bar is called Interurban. They also have the world's best corn dog.

When it comes to LGBTQ inclusion in the church there are a number of great inspiring books including, Matthew Vines *God and The Gay Christian: The Biblical Case In Support Of Same Sex Relationships*, Jeff Chu's *Does Jesus Really Love Me? A Gay Christian's Pilgrimage in Search Of God In America*, Amber Cantorna's *Refocusing My Family: Coming Out, Being Cast Out, And Discovering The True Love Of God*, Austen Hartke's *Transforming: The Bible In The Lives of Transgender Christians*, Minhee Kim-Kort's *Outside the Lines:*

How Embracing Queerness Will Transform Your Faith, and James Brownson's important Biblical-theological work *Bible, Gender, Sexuality: Reframing the Church's Debate on Same-Sex Relationships*. Also check out the work of Kathy Baldock and her work on Canyon Walker Connections. The Baptist ethicist and LGBTQ ally David Gushee was a source of deep friendship and inspiration during this time, too.

"Bad Theology Kills" was coined by Kevin Miguel García and can even be found on an awesome t-shirt at Queerly Beloved.

Ellen Page's comments were on the February 1st, 2019 episode of *The Late Show with Stephen Colbert*.

Songs of Death & Resurrection
The album that helped me get back to earth is called *Apollo: Atmospheres and Soundtracks* by Brian Eno with Daniel and Roger Lanois was first released in 1983 by EG Records.

For more on the Psalms of Ascent, check out Eugene Peterson's book *A Long Obedience in the Same Direction: Discipleship in an Instant Society*.

For more on the Hebrew Prophets read almost anything by Abraham Joshua Heschel and check out Walter Bureggemann's *Prophetic Imagination*.

The story of Mary Magdalene's encounter with the resurrected Jesus I'm talking about is in Matthew 28.

Richard Rohr's line on suffering, love and transformation is from his book *The Naked Now: Seeing As The Mystics See.* Do yourself a favor and sign up for his daily email devotional at cac.org

Choices
If you're looking to not simply fit in but belong, read Brené Brown's *Braving The Wilderness: The Quest For True Belonging And The Courage To Stand Alone.*

Henri Nouwen's wisdom on joy can be found in an edited volume called *The Heart of Henri Nouwen: His Words of Blessing.*

Yeah, go read Phyllis Tickle's book *The Great Emergence: How Christianity Is Changing and Why* and see why so much of this disruption and deconstruction makes sense in the light of history.

Check out Yo-Yo Ma's Tiny Desk Concert and conversation with Mary Louise Kelly at *NPR* from August 2018 https://www.npr.org/2018/08/17/639571356/yo-yo-ma-a-life-led-with-bach

Read up on Desmond Tutu's wisdom, in conversation with the Dalai Lama, in *The Book of Joy: Lasting Happiness in a Changing World* which was co-written with Douglas Carlton Abrams

JUSTICE

Do yourself a favor and read The *Autobiography of Nelson Mandela*. It's so good and inspiring, even though heavy at times, I'd even take it to the beach.

Getting Into Good Trouble

When it comes to learning more about Selma, watch the incredible 2014 film directed by Ava Duvernay. For more on John Lewis' story check out his 2015 memoir *Walking With The Wind: A Memoir of the Movement,* as well as the outstanding graphic novel *March* trilogy co-created with Andrew Aydin and Nate Powell.

My reflections on being arrested for immigration justice are adapted from my August 31, 2018 piece "Oregon Clergy To ICE: 'Let Our People Go!'" published on sojo.net .

I joined in with Interfaith Movement for Immigrant Justice, an Oregon group working tirelessly for immigrant rights. Immigration policy is complicated but human kindness and care for families and children should be a simple, clarion call. Read "How Trump Radicalized ICE" by Franklin Foer in the September 2018 issue of *The Atlantic.*
For biblical theology on immigration reform, check out Matthew Soerens & Jenny Yang's important book *Welcoming the Stranger: Justice, Compassion & Truth in the Immigration Debate*

Oregon Senator Jeff Merkley was one of the first elected leaders in Washington, DC to shine light on the separation of migrant children from their families as well as the fleecing of federal protective programs to implement zero tolerance immigration policy.

Holy Urgency!

Fr. Mike really believes in Jesus. So much so that he thinks Jesus might be the answer to the world's problems. On the eve of the 2000 new year's celebration, Pfleger reflected about following Jesus by being "doers of the Word" and concluded: "I pray that each one of us will have an urgency with us to reach souls for Christ, a hunger and thirst in us for God and a boldness in us to be "aggressively Christian:" presenting the witness of Christ in the workplace, the marketplace, the blocks in which we live and the schools we attend; presenting the world with the option of Jesus Christ and the standard of His Word. I pray that in doing so, the abundant blessings of God will fall upon us and be a manifestation to all, of God's unconditional love for His children and their faithfulness." For more on Father Pleger read "Father Mike: A militant white priest fights for his black parishioners on the South Side" by Evan Osnos in the February 29, 2016 issue of the *New Yorker* as well as my friend Cathleen Falsani's excellent piece "The Michael Pfleger I Know" published by *Religion News Service* on June 10, 2008.

This Is Not The End, This Is the Revealing
Ched Myers wrote my favorite breakdown of the Gospel of
Mark in a book called *Binding the Strong Man: A Political
Reading of Mark's Story of Jesus*. He regularly blogs
at radicaldiscipleship.net where I came across his quote on
climate change.

The gathering in Thailand was called Mesa Friends and was
in October 2014, co-convened by Brian McLaren, Steve
Chalke, and organized by Carolyn and Fuzz Kitto. To learn
more about Oasis's "ethos" listen to Jill Rowe's conversation
with Rob Bell on Robcast #127

I'm Dying To See How This One Ends - A Postscript
You can read about Melania Trump's 2014 Facebook post
and Taylor Swift's 2016 comments over at bustle.com/p/
video-of-trump-playing-taylor-swifts-blank-space-in-his-rolls-
royce-has-resurfaced-12204667

Gratitudes

Desmond Tutu reminds us that "I am because we are."

Deep wells of gratitude to Ali and Charlie Moore, Amy and Christian Piatt, Andy and Amy Goebel, Paul and Marcia Corner, Darsey and Brian Landoe, Kazi Joshua, Phillis Sheppard, Phil Anderson, Stephen Hendrickson and David McCord, Benj and Marit Ecker, Cathleen Falsani and Maurice Possley, David and Sarah Vanderveen, Glenn Rogers and Iris Bourne, Wes Granberg-Michaelson, Nicole Tignor, Elsa Johnson, Amy Wolf, Emily and Sam Leach, Jessica Ferrell, Pat and Roy Smithey, Nathan and Kristen Rix, Sindy and Andrea Vasquez, Chris Hamel and Banning Hendricks, Pat and Kathy Sullivan, Chinweike Eseonu, Kaitlyn and Mitch Winn, Jennifer Greenberg, Jess Calvert and Matt Freeman, Matt Johnson, Boris and Abbey Lustovsky, Justin Kent, Roland Conrad, Molly and Tom, Jana and Gavin Dluehosh, Ryan and Jeana Wines, Ben and Jen Lindwall, James and Kate Rohl, Kurt Kroon, Sarah Schwartzendruber, Insil Kang, Cory Doiron, Julia Nielsen, Nathan LeRud, Melissa Reed, Ron Werner Jr, Michael Ellick, Sara Roseneau, Erin Martin, Zeb Highben (for dragging me to that Bonhoeffer study 20+ years ago), Stan Mitchell, Jon Gettings, Michael Hidalgo, Dave Neuhausel, Paula Williams, Jonathan Williams, Mark Tidd, Jenny Morgan, Rachael McClair, Laura Truax, Todd Johnson, Jay Phelan, Fred Davie, Josh Dickson, Derrick Harkins, Fred Harrell, George Mekhail, Ryan Meeks, Scott Erickson, Justin Zoradi, Chase and Melissa Reeves, The Meyer Family expanded lunch bunch, George Lee, Jayme Cloninger, Joel Griffith, Justin Fung, Meighan Stone, Brit Barron and Sami Cromelin, Candice Czubernat, The JMS Beale, Lenore and Aaron

Johnson, Patrick and Megan Carmitchel, Nasr and the Odeh's, Larry and Mary Kay Prior (especially for taking me to my first mass way back when), Joshua and Katie Templeton, Taryn Markee, Jack Kennedy, Karen Nettler, John Calhoun, Mary Ann and John McComb, Margaret McDonnell, Matthew Frazier, Ken Weber, Matt Higginson, Steve Chalke, Jill Rowe, Dave Parr, Joy Madeiros, Dan Dowman, Jim Wallis, Brian McLaren, Cameron Trimble, Lisa Sharon Harper, Rob Bell, Martin Wroe, Father Richard Rohr, Michael Poffenberger, Tim King, Ashley and Chris LaTondresse.

All of our Christ Church: Portland people near and far.

My family.

Sarah and Des.

57298798R00090

Made in the USA
Middletown, DE
30 July 2019